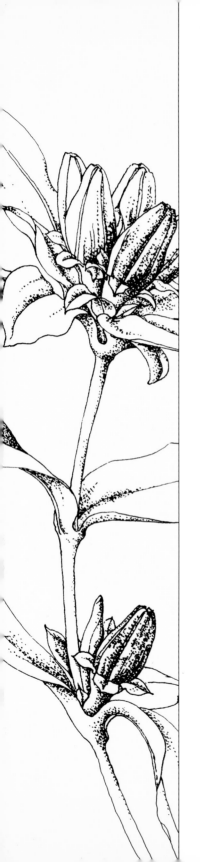

WILDFLOWERS
OF MASSACHUSETTS, CONNECTICUT, AND RHODE ISLAND

IN COLOR

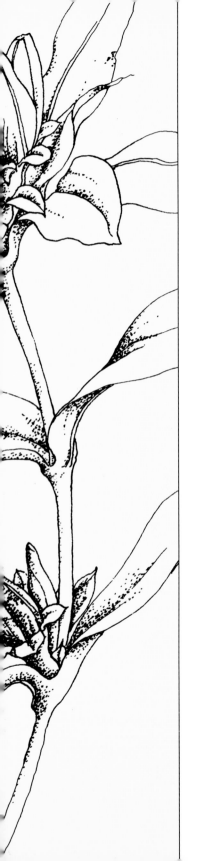

WILDFLOWERS
OF MASSACHUSETTS, CONNECTICUT, AND RHODE ISLAND

IN COLOR

WILLIAM K. CHAPMAN
VALERIE CONLEY CHAPMAN
ALAN E. BESSETTE
ARLEEN RAINIS BESSETTE

BOTANICAL DRAWINGS BY
PHILIPPA BROWN

Syracuse University Press

For a listing of books published and distributed by Syracuse University Press,
visit our Web site at SyracuseUniversityPress.syr.edu.

ISBN-13: 978-0-8156-3185-9 (cl.)
ISBN-10: 0-8156-3185-5 (cl.)
ISBN-13: 978-0-8156-0926-1 (pbk.)
ISBN-10: 0-8156-0926-4 (pbk.)

Library of Congress Cataloging-in-Publication Data

Wildflowers of Massachusetts, Connecticut, and Rhode Island in color /
William K. Chapman ... [et al.] ; botanical drawings by Philippa Brown.   1st ed.
          p.   cm.
    Includes index.
    ISBN 978−0−8156−3185−9 (cloth : alk. paper)
    — ISBN 978−0−8156−0926−1 (pbk.: alk. paper)
    1. Wild flowers Massachusetts Identification.
    2. Wild flowers Connecticut Identification.
    3. Wild flowers Rhode Island Identification.
    4. Wild flowers Massachusetts Pictorical works.
    5. Wild flowers Connecticut Pictorical works.
    6. Wild flowers Rhode Island Pictorical works.
    I. Chapman, William K., 1951
    QK166.W54   2008
    582.13'0974—dc21
    2007052079

Preceding page: Bottle gentian, gentiana clausa

Manufactured in Hong Kong through AmericanBook.Net
Series / Book Design by CRISTINA LAZAR

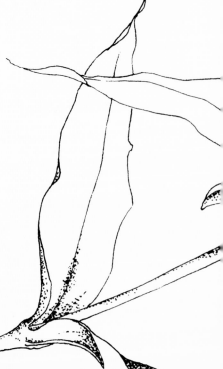

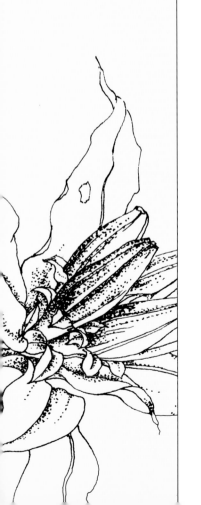

This book is dedicated to the memory of
Valerie Chapman (1953–2007),
beloved wife and companion of William Chapman.

❧

CONTENTS

ACKNOWLEDGMENTS

The authors wish to acknowledge the many people who have contributed valuable time and effort in the creation of this book. The Revised Checklist of New York State Plants by Richard S. Mitchell and Gordon C. Tucker served as our primary reference source for nomenclature and terminology. Our sincere thanks to the following people who by way of written correspondence, telephone conversations, or guided walks assisted us in locating selected wildflowers: Paul Martin Brown, Evelyn Greene, Brian Reed, Richard Porcher, Joseph and Betsy Strauch, Richard Mitchell, Charles Sheviak, Steve Young, Mario DiGregorio, and Ronald Stewart. The beautiful illustration of Blue Curls was kindly provided by Joseph Strauch. Stu and Brenda Card, Alan Smith, Cheryl Anderson, and Vicky Marcy provided essential technical assistance in the preparation of this manuscript. We thank Philippa Brown for providing the botanical drawings. We are especially grateful to Alice Randel Pfeiffer and her staff at Syracuse University Press who made this book possible.

HOW TO USE THIS GUIDE

We have prepared this field guide to make identifying unfamiliar flowers as easy a process as possible. By following the simple procedure described below, you will be able to identify the wildflowers described in this book in a matter of minutes simply by making choices having to do with a few easily differentiated characteristics.

The first characteristic to consider is *color*. Is the flower white? After white, the other choices are the colors of the rainbow. This guide follows the example of nature and lists those colors in the same order that they are displayed across the sky after a storm, beginning with red and continuing through violet. Within the spectrum, the color that is somewhat problematic and causes the greatest concern is purple. Purple flowers with a predominant bluish cast have been included in the blue-to-violet category. All the species whose color appears to have been visibly influenced by any degree or shade of pink-to-red pigmentation have been included in the pink-to-red category. The final color choice encompasses the darkest colors to be found on flowers, those ranging from deep purple to brown. Occasionally, a flower is found that is such a dark shade of purple that it first appears to be nearly black. However, we are not aware of any truly black wildflower.

One final note on identifying flower colors: In some flowers the color of the petals or the petal-like parts differs from the color of the disc, or center, of the bloom. In such cases, we have assigned that species to a color category according to the color of the petals.

After you determine the color of a wildflower, the next step is to examine the *physical structure of the flower*. Is the flower radially symmetrical or nearly so? Radially symmetrical flowers have petals or petal-like parts that extend outward from the center of the flower more or less evenly in all directions, like a daisy. (The term "petals or petal-like parts" is used throughout this guide to refer to any floral usually colorful parts that appear to be a petal, even though technically these parts may be sepals, modified bracts, and so on). If a flower is radially symmetrical, you should then count the number of petals or petal-like parts. The possible categories range from 3 to 7 or more petals or petal-like parts. A few species, such as goldthread or bloodroot, typically exhibit variations in the number of petals per bloom. In these cases we have relied on personal experience in assigning such species to the category that is most appropriate.

Following the 5 categories of radially symmetrical flowers is the final possible selection, a catchall classification for any wildflowers not fitting into the previous categories. Flowers in this grouping do not appear to be radially symmetrical. They may have fewer than 3 petals or petal-like parts or flowers that are minute, filamentous, tubular with no or uneven petal-like lobes or with no obvious petals or petal-like parts. If a flower is tubular to dish-shaped with a number of conspicuous symmetrical, petal-like lobes, then that species will be found in the radially symmetrical category. If the flower is tubular but the lobes (or "teeth") are unequal in size and shape or minute, then that species will be found in the asymmetrical category.

After you determine the color and structure of the flower, the next step is to examine the leaves. The *leaf arrangement* on the plant should fall into one of the following categories: *(1)* aquatic,* *(2)* leaves lacking, *(3)* leaves basal, *(4)* leaves alternate, or *(5)* leaves opposite or whorled.

In some species leaf arrangements may include two categories, such as having both basal and alternate leaves on the same plant. In these cases the plant is assigned to a category according to which leaves appear to be the more prominent. You should also take leaf arrangement to mean the way the leaves would appear at first glance to the average person encountering the plant for the first time. For example, several species have trailing or subterranean stems that put up leaves and flowers at intervals. If the leaves of such plants appear basal, then that is the category in which they are included.

---

*Although "aquatic" is not a true leaf arrangement, it is a useful category for simplifying the identification process.

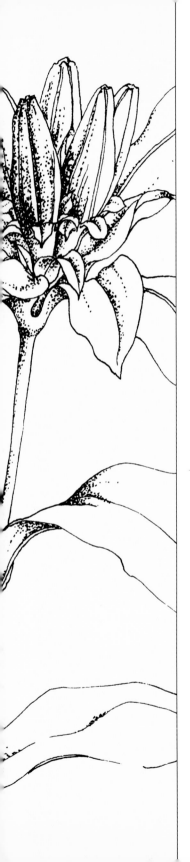

PART ONE

WHITE FLOWERS

❧

FLOWERS SYMMETRICAL, WITH 3 PETALS OR PETAL-LIKE PARTS

LEAVES BASAL, SIMPLE

Arrowhead, Wapato
•*Sagittaria latifolia* Willd.
•Water-plantain family **Alismataceae**
FLOWERING SEASON: July–August. FLOWERS: white with a yellow center, in whorls of 3 on a loosely flowered upright stem; about 1¼" (3.1 cm) wide, with 3 rounded petals. PLANT: aquatic, 4–36" (10–91 cm) tall; leaves basal, erect, simple, arrowhead-shaped, long-stalked, margin entire, green. HABITAT: shallow water. COMMENTS: several other species of *Sagittaria*, some with very narrow leaves, also occur in this region.

Snowdrop
•*Galanthus nivalis* L.
•Lily family **Liliaceae**
FLOWERING SEASON: March–April. FLOWERS: white with inner green markings, solitary, terminal; ¾–1" (1.9–2.5 cm) wide, with 3 spreading rounded petal-like parts surrounding a smaller protruding center, nodding. PLANT: 3–7" (7.5–17.5 cm) tall; leaves appearing basal, simple, long and narrow, margin entire, green. HABITAT: woodlands, thickets. COMMENTS: persisting and spreading from cultivation.

LEAVES WHORLED, SIMPLE

White Trillium
•*Trillium grandiflorum*
  (Michx.) Salisb.
•Lily family **Liliaceae**
FLOWERING SEASON: late April through May. FLOWER: white, becoming pink just before wilting, solitary and terminal on a tall erect stalk; about 3" (7.5 cm) wide, with 3 large, evenly whorled petals, petals ovate with a tapering, pointed tip, often slightly recurved. PLANT: 8–18" (20–45 cm) tall; leaves 3, in a whorl at the base of the flower stalk, simple, ovate with a tapering, pointed tip and an entire margin, practically stalkless, green. HABITAT: woodlands. COMMENTS: the name trillium refers to three, the number of leaves, sepals, and petals.

Painted Trillium
•*Trillium undulatum* Willd.
•Lily family **Liliaceae**
FLOWERING SEASON: May. FLOWER: white with crimson veins around the center, solitary and terminal on an erect stalk; about 2" (5 cm) wide, with 3 evenly whorled petals, petals lance-shaped with a tapering, pointed tip. PLANT: 8–24" (20–60 cm) tall; leaves 3, in a whorl at the base of the flower stalk, simple, ovate with a tapering, pointed tip and an entire margin, short-stalked, green. HABITAT: woodlands.

Nodding Trillium
•*Trillium cernuum* L.
•Lily family **Liliaceae**
FLOWERING SEASON: mid-May to mid-June. FLOWER: white, solitary and terminal on a drooping stalk characteristically oriented below the leaves, with 3 evenly whorled petals; petals about 1" (2.5 cm) long, broadly lance-shaped, deeply recurved. PLANT: 8–20" (20–50 cm) tall; leaves 3, in a whorl at the base of the flower stalk, simple, broadly ovate with a pointed tip and an entire margin, stalkless or nearly so, green. HABITAT: moist woodlands, wooded swamps.

White Trillium / *Trillium grandiflorum*

Arrowhead, Wapato / *Sagittaria latifolia*

Painted Trillium / *Trillium undulatum*

Nodding Trillium / *Trillium cernuum*

Snowdrop / *Galanthus nivalis*

FLOWERS SYMMETRICAL, WITH 4 PETALS OR PETAL-LIKE PARTS

LEAVES ALTERNATE, SIMPLE

Garlic Mustard
•*Alliaria petiolata*
 (Bieb.) Cav. and Grande
•Mustard family **Brassicaceae**
FLOWERING SEASON: May. FLOWERS: white, few to several in a terminal cluster; about 5/16" (8 mm) wide, cross-shaped, with 4 narrowly oval petals. PLANT: 1–3' (30–90 cm) tall; leaves alternate, simple, heart-shaped to triangular, margin coarsely toothed, green; seedpods 1–2" (2.5–5 cm) long, very slender. HABITAT: roadsides, waste areas, fields, and woodlands. COMMENTS: crushed leaves have a garlic-like odor.

Field Pennycress
•*Thlaspi arvense* L.
•Mustard family **Brassicaceae**
FLOWERING SEASON: early May to mid-June. FLOWERS: white, several to many in a terminal cluster; about 1/16" (2 mm) wide, cross-shaped, with 4 oval petals. PLANT: 6–18" (15–46 cm) tall; leaves alternate, simple, lance-shaped, often clasping the stem, margin toothed, green; seedpods about 3/8" (1 cm) long, oval with a notched tip, flattened. HABITAT: fields and waste places.

Wild Peppergrass
•*Lepidium virginicum* L.
•Mustard family **Brassicaceae**
FLOWERING SEASON: mid-May to July. FLOWERS: white, many in slender terminal clusters; about 1/16" (1.6 mm) wide, cross-shaped, with 4 oval petals. PLANT: 6–24" (15–60 cm) tall; leaves alternate and basal, simple; upper leaves lance-shaped, margin sharply toothed or entire; basal leaves obovate with tiny lobes along the stalk, margin toothed, green; seedpods about 5/8" (1.6 cm) long, nearly round, notched. HABITAT: fields and roadsides. COMMENTS: field-cress, *Lepidium campestre*, has oblong to paddle-shaped basal leaves and narrowly arrowhead-shaped stem leaves.

Sea-rocket
•*Cakile edentula* (Bigel.) Hook.
•Mustard family **Brassicaceae**
FLOWERING SEASON: July–August. FLOWERS: white to pale purple, few in a terminal cluster; about 1/4" (5 mm) wide, cross-shaped, with 4 oval petals. PLANT: 8–12" (20–30 cm) tall; leaves alternate, simple, lance-shaped, margin unevenly toothed, green; seedpods 1/2–3/4" (1.3–1.9 cm) long, 2-sectioned, upper section slightly larger, ovoid. HABITAT: coastal sandy soil, also along Lake Erie.

Large Cranberry
•*Vaccinium macrocarpon* Ait.
•Heath family **Ericaceae**
FLOWERING SEASON: mid-June–July. FLOWERS: white to pinkish white with a brownish cone-shaped center, many, axial; about 5/16" (8 mm) wide, tubular with 4 narrow, deeply recurved, petal-like lobes. PLANT: woody, branched, trailing; leaves alternate, simple, oblong, small, margin entire, green; fruit an acidic, ovoid red berry, edible. HABITAT: bogs, fen meadows.

Sea-rocket / *Cakile edentula*

Large Cranberry / *Vaccinium macrocarpon*

Wild Peppergrass / *Lepidium virginicum*

Field Pennycress / *Thlaspi arvense*

Garlic Mustard / *Alliaria petiolata*

Canadian Mayflower
- *Maianthemum canadense* Desf.
- Lily family Liliaceae

FLOWERING SEASON: late May to late June. FLOWERS: white, up to 20 in an oval terminal cluster 1–2" (2.5–5 cm) long; individual flowers about ³⁄₁₆" (5 mm) wide, with 4 oblong petal-like parts. PLANT: 2–7" (5–17.5 cm) tall; leaves usually 2, alternate, simple, somewhat heart-shaped, margin entire, green, glossy. HABITAT: woodlands. COMMENTS: unusual in that most members of the lily family have perianth parts in multiples of 3. Also known as the false or wild lily-of-the-valley.

LEAVES ALTERNATE, COMPOUND OR DEEPLY DIVIDED

Cut-leaf Toothwort
- *Cardamine concatenata* (Michx.) Schwein
- Mustard family Brassicaceae

FLOWERING SEASON: late April to mid-May. FLOWERS: white, few to several, in a terminal cluster; about ⅝" (1.6 cm) wide, cross-shaped, with 4 oval petals. PLANT: 8–15" (20–37.5 cm) tall; leaves alternate, deeply divided, margin coarsely toothed, green; seedpods 1–1½" (2.5–3.8 cm) long, slender, spreading. HABITAT: woodlands. COMMENTS: two-leaf toothwort, *Cardamine diphylla*, which blooms just after the cut-leaf toothwort, has leaves with 3 broad ovate divisions.

Cuckoo-flower
- *Cardamine pratensis* L.
- Mustard family Brassicaceae

FLOWERING SEASON: May–June. FLOWERS: white, sometimes tinged with lilac, few to several in a slender terminal cluster; ½–¾" (1.3–1.9 cm) wide, with 4 rounded petals. PLANT: 8–20" (20–50 cm) tall; leaves alternate and basal, pinnately compound; margins entire or toothed, green. HABITAT: wet meadows, swamps.

Watercress
- *Rorippa nasturtium-aquaticum* (L.) Hayek
- Mustard family Brassicaceae

FLOWERING SEASON: June into August. FLOWERS: white, several in terminal clusters; about ³⁄₁₆" (5 mm) wide, cross-shaped, with 4 oval petals. PLANT: aquatic; leaves alternate, pinnately compound with 3–9 segments, margins uneven, green; seedpods about 1" (2.5 cm) long, slender, long-stalked, spreading. HABITAT: in brooks, streams, and drainage ditches.

LEAVES OPPOSITE OR WHORLED, SIMPLE

Bunchberry
- *Cornus canadensis* L.
- Dogwood family Cornaceae

FLOWERING SEASON: June. FLOWERHEAD: white with a greenish center, about 1" (2.5 cm) wide, rimmed by 4–6 large white petal-like bracts; individual flowers tiny, greenish, with 4 minute petals. PLANT: 3–9" (7.5–22.5 cm) tall; leaves whorled, simple, ovate with a pointed tip, margin entire, green; fruit a ¼" (6 mm) wide "bunched cluster" of smooth bright-red berries. HABITAT: woodlands.

Sweet-scented Bedstraw
- *Galium triflorum* Michx.
- Madder family Rubiaceae

FLOWERING SEASON: June–July. FLOWERS: white to greenish white, many in 3-branched terminal and axial clusters; tiny, corolla with 4 sharply pointed, petal-like lobes. PLANT: 1–3' (30–90 cm) tall; leaves whorled in groups of 6 on a smooth stalk, simple, narrowly oval, margin entire, green. HABITAT: fields and

Bunchberry / *Cornus canadensis*

Watercress / *Rorippa nasturtium-aquaticum*

Cut-leaf Toothwort / *Cardamine concatenata*

Sweet-scented Bedstraw / *Galium triflorum*

Canadian Mayflower / *Maianthemum canadense*

Cuckoo-flower / *Cardamine pratensis*

waste areas. COMMENTS: goosegrass, *Galium aparine*, has a spiny stem, rough leaves, and small clusters of axial flowers.

Partridge-berry, Twin-berry
•*Mitchella repens* L.
•Madder family **Rubiaceae**
FLOWERING SEASON: late June–July. FLOWERS: white, in terminal pairs; up to ½" (1.3 cm) long, tubular with 4 pointed and often recurved, petal-like lobes. PLANT: prostrate; leaves opposite on 6–12" (15–30 cm) long stems, simple, nearly round, margin entire, green, often with whitish veining, evergreen. HABITAT: woodlands. COMMENTS: the bright-red berries are edible but bland.

LEAVES OPPOSITE, COMPOUND

Virgin's-bower
•*Clematis virginiana* L.
•Crowfoot family **Ranunculaceae**
FLOWERING SEASON: late July–August. FLOWERS: white, several in showy axial clusters; about 1" (2.5 cm) wide, with 4 narrowly oblong petal-like sepals and numerous prominent thread-like stamens. PLANT: a climbing vine up to 10' (3 m) long; leaves opposite, with 3 lance-shaped occasionally lobed leaflets, margins unevenly toothed, green. HABITAT: open woodlands, hedgerows, and wooded swamps. COMMENTS: this species produces showy clusters of plumed seeds.

FLOWERS SYMMETRICAL, WITH 5 PETALS OR PETAL-LIKE PARTS

LACKING TYPICAL LEAVES

Dodder
•*Cuscuta gronovii* Willd. ex Schultz
•Dodder family **Cuscutaceae**
FLOWERING SEASON: July–September. FLOWERS: white, many, in densely flow-ered clusters all along the stems; about ⅛–¼" (3–6 mm) wide, bell-shaped with 5 petal-like lobes. PLANT: vine-like, trailing and climbing over adjacent vegetation; leaves lacking; stems orange to yellow. HABITAT: moist soil adjoining bodies of water.

AQUATIC, LEAVES FLOATING

Floating-heart
•*Nymphoides cordata* (Ell.) Fern.
•Buckbean family **Menyanthaceae**
FLOWERING SEASON: June–September. FLOWERS: white, several, terminal on individual stalks; ¼–½" (0.6–13 mm) wide, with 5 petals. PLANT: aquatic; leaves floating, simple, somewhat heart-shaped, margin entire, green. HABITAT: ponds.

LEAVES BASAL, SIMPLE

Spathulate-leaved Sundew
•*Drosera intermedia* Hayne
•Sundew family **Droseraceae**
FLOWERING SEASON: July into August. FLOWERS: white, several, in a slender terminal cluster; about ¼" (6 mm) wide, with 5 oblong petals. PLANT: 3–8" (7.5–20 cm) tall; leaves basal, simple, spoon-shaped with long stalks, upper surface covered with reddish glandular hairs with a sticky, syrup-like coating, margin entire, green. HABITAT: bogs, fens, and wet sand. COMMENTS: a carnivorous plant that uses its sticky hairs to entrap insects. Round-leaved sundew, *Drosera rotundifolia*, has nearly round leaves, whereas thread-leaved sundew, *D. filiformis*, has long, narrow, thread-like leaves.

Dodder / *Cuscuta gronovii*

Virgin's-bower / *Clematis virginiana*

Spathulate-leaved Sundew / *Drosera intermedia*

Floating-heart / *Nymphoides cordata*

Partridge-berry, Twin-berry / *Mitchella repens*

Round-leaf Pyrola, Shinleaf

• *Pyrola americana* Sweet
• Heath family **Ericaceae**

FLOWERING SEASON: late June–July. FLOWERS: white, several to many on a spike-like terminal cluster; about ¾" (1.9 cm) wide, with 5 rounded petals, nodding. PLANT: 6–20" (15–50 cm) tall; leaves basal, simple, nearly round, margin minutely toothed, green. HABITAT: woodlands.

One-flowered Pyrola, One-flowered Wintergreen

• *Moneses uniflora* (L.) Gray
• Heath family **Ericaceae**

FLOWERING SEASON: mid-June to early July. FLOWERS: white, solitary, terminal; about ¾" (2 cm) wide, with 5 broad petals. PLANT: 2–6" (5–15.5 cm) tall; leaves 2–6, opposite or whorled but appearing basal, simple, rounded to ovate, margin with minute rounded teeth, green. HABITAT: woodlands.

Early Saxifrage

• *Saxifraga virginiensis* Michx.
• Saxifrage family **Saxifragaceae**

FLOWERING SEASON: late April–May. FLOWERS: white, many on a branched terminal cluster; up to ¼" (6 mm) wide, with 5 rounded petals. PLANT: 4–12" (10–30 cm) tall; leaves mostly basal, simple, ovate with a bluntly toothed margin, green. HABITAT: rocky, usually moist soils, often on wet cliffs.

Grass-of-Parnassus

• *Parnassia glauca* Raf.
• Saxifrage family **Saxifragaceae**

FLOWERING SEASON: August–September. FLOWER: white with greenish veins, solitary, terminal; about 1" (2.5 cm) wide, with 5 oval petals. PLANT: 8–24" (20–60 cm) tall; leaves mostly basal, with 1 on the stem, simple, broadly egg-shaped to nearly round, margin entire, green.

HABITAT: swamps and moist meadows.

Foamflower

• *Tiarella cordifolia* L.
• Saxifrage family **Saxifragaceae**

FLOWERING SEASON: mid-May to mid-June. FLOWERS: white, about a dozen in a narrow terminal cluster; about ¼" (6 mm) wide, with 5 narrow petals and 10 long conspicuous stamens that give the flower a feathery appearance. PLANT: 6–12" (15–30 cm) tall; leaves basal, simple, heart-shaped with 3–7 angular lobes, margins toothed, green. HABITAT: woodlands.

Dewdrop, False Violet

• *Dalibarda repens* L.
• Rose family **Rosaceae**

FLOWERING SEASON: late July to mid-August. FLOWERS: white, 1 or 2 arising in leaf axils; about ⅜" (9 mm) wide, with 5 rounded petals. PLANT: creeping, 2–6" (5–15 cm) long; leaves basal, simple, heart-shaped, margin scalloped, pubescent on both sides, green. HABITAT: open woodlands and fen borders.

One-flowered Pyrola, One-flowered Wintergreen / *Moneses uniflora*

Round-leaf Pyrola / *Pyrola americana*

Early Saxifrage / *Saxifraga virginiensis*

Foamflower / *Tiarella cordifolia*

Dewdrop, False Violet / *Dalibarda repens*

Grass-of-Parnassus / *Parnassia glauca*

LEAVES BASAL, COMPOUND

Goldthread

- *Coptis trifolia* (L.) Salisb.
- Crowfoot family **Ranunculaceae**

FLOWERING SEASON: May.   FLOWER: white, solitary, terminal; about ½" (1.3 cm) wide, with 5–7 lance-shaped, petal-like sepals.   PLANT: 3–6" (7.5–15 cm) tall; leaves basal, long-stalked, compound with 3 fan-shaped, sharply toothed leaflets, green, glossy, evergreen. HABITAT: damp woods.   COMMENTS: named for its slender yellow-orange roots.

Wild Strawberry

- *Fragaria virginiana* Mill
- Rose family **Rosaceae**

FLOWERING SEASON: May.   FLOWERS: white with a yellow center, few, in a terminal cluster; about ¾" (1.9 cm) wide, with 5 rounded petals.   PLANT: creeping, 3–6" (7.5–15 cm) tall; leaves appearing basal, 3-lobed; leaflets broadly oval to obovate, margins toothed, green; fruit red, ovoid, fragrant, edible.   HABITAT: fields and edges of woodlands.

Common Wood-sorrel

- *Oxalis acetosella* L.
- Oxalis family **Oxalidaceae**

FLOWERING SEASON: late May–July. FLOWERS: pinkish white to white with dark-pink veins, solitary to several in leaf axils; about ¾" (1.9 cm) wide, with 5 rounded petals.   PLANT: 2–6" (5–15 cm) tall; leaves appearing basal, compound with 3 leaflets; leaflets heart-shaped, margin entire, green.   HABITAT: moist woodlands.

Buckbean, Bogbean

- *Menyanthes trifoliata* L.
- Buckbean family **Menyanthaceae**

FLOWERING SEASON: late May to early June.   FLOWERS: white, several to many in a terminal cluster; about ½" (1.3 cm) long, tubular with 5 spreading, hairy, petal-like lobes.   PLANT: 4–8" (10–20 cm) tall; leaves basal, with three leaflets; leaflets obovate, margins entire, green.   HABITAT: bogs, fens, and along ponds.

LEAVES ALTERNATE, SIMPLE

Poke, Pokeweed

- *Phytolacca americana* L.
- Pokeweed family **Phytolaccaceae**

FLOWERING SEASON: July to early August. FLOWERS: white with a green center, many on slender 2–8" (5–20 cm) long, loosely flowered terminal and axial clusters; up to ¼" (6 mm) wide, with 5 rounded, petal-like divisions.   PLANT: 4–12' (1.2–3.6 m) tall; leaves alternate on a purplish stem, large, simple, broadly lance-shaped, margin entire, green; fruit a grape-like cluster of very dark-purple inedible berries.   HABITAT: meadows and woodlots.

Japanese Knotweed, Japanese Bamboo

- *Polygonum cuspidatum* Sieb. and Zucc.
- Buckwheat family **Polygonaceae**

FLOWERING SEASON: mid-August–September.   FLOWERS: white, many in slender, 2–4" (5–10 cm) long terminal and upper axial clusters; minute, with 5 petal-like lobes.   PLANT: 4–8' (1.2–2.4 m) tall; appearing shrub-like but stems not perennial; leaves alternate on a bamboo-like stem, simple, broadly ovate with a somewhat squared base, margin entire, green.   HABITAT: fields, waste areas, roadsides, thickets, and moist soil.

Goldthread / *Coptis trifolia*

Buckbean, Bogbean / *Menyanthes trifolata*

Poke, Pokeweed / *Phytolacca americana*

Wild Strawberry / *Fragaria virginiana*

Common Wood-sorrel / *Oxalis acetosella*

Japanese Knotweed, Japanese Bamboo /
Polygonum cuspidatum

Marsh-mallow
•*Althaea officinalis* L.
•Mallow family **Malvaceae**
FLOWERING SEASON: July–September.
FLOWERS: off-white to pinkish white, several, in few flowered terminal and axillary clusters; about 1–1½" (2.5–3.8 cm) wide, with 5 broad petals. PLANT: 2–4½' (0.6–1.4 m) tall; leaves simple, alternate, ovate and somewhat 3-lobed, margin toothed, green, covered with a pale pubescence.   HABITAT: coastal salt marshes. COMMENTS: the root was the original source of the popular campfire confection.

Cheese Mallow
•*Malva neglecta* Wallr.
•Mallow family **Malvaceae**
FLOWERING SEASON: June–August.
FLOWERS: whitish with lavender veins, sometimes with a bluish tinge, 1 to several, in axils along the stem; about ½" (1.3 cm) wide with 5 broad petals notched at the tip. PLANT: 4–12" (10–30 cm) long, mostly prostrate; leaves alternate, simple, heart-shaped with a rounded tip, shallowly lobed, margin scalloped to somewhat toothed, green. HABITAT: fields and waste areas. COMMENTS: called cheeses in reference to the wheel-shaped fruit.

Labrador Tea
•*Rhododendron groenlandicum*
   (Oeder) Kron and Judd
•Heath family **Ericaceae**
FLOWERING SEASON: June.   FLOWERS: white, several to many in a rounded terminal cluster; ¼–⅜" (6–9 mm) wide, tubular at the base with 5 spreading, petal-like lobes. PLANT: shrub, about 1–3' (30–90 cm) tall; leaves alternate, simple, oblong with an inrolled margin, dark green above, downy and white (young leaves) to rusty (mature leaves) below, evergreen. HABITAT: bogs, fens, swamps, and drier acidic soils. COMMENTS: specimens growing at higher elevations are often stunted.

Great Laurel
•*Rhododendron maximum* L.
•Heath family **Ericaceae**
FLOWERING SEASON: July.   FLOWERS: white to pale pink, with a sprinkling of gold-green dots on the inner surface, many in large globular terminal clusters; ¾–1¼" (2–3 cm) wide, tubular at the base with 5 large oval petal-like lobes. PLANT: a shrub, 3–15' (0.9–4.6 m) or more high; leaves alternate, simple, large, oblong to lance-shaped, margin entire and often curled, green, evergreen. HABITAT: shaded, moist soils, along streams.

Mountain Laurel
•*Kalmia latifolia* L.
•Heath family **Ericaceae**
FLOWERING SEASON: mid-June to mid-July. FLOWERS: white to pinkish, many, in a spherical terminal cluster; ¾–1" (1.9–2.5 cm) wide, saucer-shaped with 5 shallowly pointed lobes. PLANT: shrub, 5–15' (1.5–4.6 m) tall; leaves alternate, simple, lance-shaped with an entire margin, green, evergreen. HABITAT: in sandy or rocky soil in woodlands. COMMENTS: *bees visiting these flowers are said to produce poisonous honey.*

Trailing Arbutus
•*Epigaea repens* L.
•Heath family **Ericaceae**
FLOWERING SEASON: mid-April to mid-May. FLOWERS: white to pink, several, in a terminal cluster; about ½" (1.3 cm) wide, tubular at the base with 5 spreading, petal-like lobes; fragrant. PLANT: prostrate on the ground; leaves alternate along a hairy woody stem, simple, oval with an entire margin, green, evergreen. HABITAT: sandy or rocky woods, especially under evergreens.

Great Laurel / *Rhododendron maximum*

Cheese Mallow / *Malva neglecta*

Mountain Laurel / *Kalmia latifolia*

Labrador Tea / *Rhododendron groenlandicum*

Marsh-mallow / *Althaea officinalis*

Trailing Arbutus / *Epigaea repens*

Beach Plum
- *Prunus maritima* Marsh.
- Rose family **Rosaceae**

FLOWERING SEASON: May–early June. FLOWERS: white, many, in several flowered clusters along the branches; about ⅔" (1.6 cm) broad, with 5 obovate petals. PLANT: shrub, 1–7' (0.3–2.1 m) tall; leaves alternate, simple, oval to ovate to obovate, margin toothed, green; fruit purple, about ¾" (1.9 cm) wide, containing a single seed, edible. HABITAT: beaches and sandy soils near the coast.

Sand Cherry
- *Prunus pumila* L.
- Rose family **Rosaceae**

FLOWERING SEASON: May–early June. FLOWERS: white, several, in few flowered clusters along the branches; about ⅓" (8.3 mm) wide, with 5 rounded petals. PLANT: trailing shrub, ½–5' (0.15–1.5 m) tall; leaves alternate, simple, narrowly oblanceolate to spathulate, margin toothed, green. HABITAT: sandy or gravelly soils, usually bordering waterways.

Meadow-sweet
- *Spiraea latifolia* (Ait.) Borkh.
- Rose family **Rosaceae**

FLOWERING SEASON: July to mid-August. FLOWERS: white with pinkish centers, many in showy upright, 3–5" (7.5–12.5 cm) terminal and axial clusters; about 5⁄16" (8 mm) wide, with 5 rounded petals. PLANT: shrub, 2–5' (0.6–1.5 m) tall; leaves alternate, simple, oblong, margin coarsely and unevenly toothed, green. HABITAT: swamps, meadows, and roadsides.

Red Chokeberry
- *Aronia arbutifolia* (L.) Pers.
- Rose family **Rosaceae**

FLOWERING SEASON: mid-May to mid-June. FLOWERS: white, many in rounded terminal clusters; about ½" (1.2 cm) wide, with 5 rounded petals. PLANT: shrub, 3–8' (0.9–2.4 m) tall; leaves alternate, simple, oval to obovate, margin toothed, green; fruit about ¼" (6 mm) long, apple-like, red, with astringent flesh. HABITAT: moist thickets and drier sandy soils.

Kiwi, Hardy Kiwi
- *Actinidia arguta* Sieb. and Zucc.
- Kiwi family **Actinidiaceae**

FLOWERING SEASON: June. FLOWERS: white with a pale-green globular center, many, occurring singly or in small axillary clusters; about ¾–1" (1.9–2.5 cm) wide, with 5 rounded petals. PLANT: woody vine; leaves alternate, simple, broadly heart-shaped, margin finely toothed, green; leaf stalk frequently scarlet. HABITAT: woodlands, originally persisting or spreading from cultivation. COMMENTS: to the best of the authors' knowledge, wild populations are known only from Berkshire County in Massachusetts. Capable of choking out adjacent vegetation, this species could become a serious pest if its range becomes more extensive. At a distance, easily misidentified as oriental bittersweet *(Celastrus orbiculata)*.

New Jersey Tea
- *Ceanothus americanus* L.
- Buckthorn family **Rhamnaceae**

FLOWERING SEASON: July. FLOWERS: white, many in rounded terminal and long-stalked axial clusters; minute, with 5 tiny petals. PLANT: shrub, 2–4' (0.6–1.2 m) tall; leaves alternate, simple, ovate with a pointed tip, margin toothed, green. HABITAT: woodlands.

Beach Plum / *Prunus maritima*

Red Chokeberry / *Aronia arbutifolia*

New Jersey Tea / *Ceanothus americanus*

Sand Cherry / *Prunus pumila*

Kiwi, Hardy Kiwi / *Actinidia arguta*

Meadow-sweet / *Spiraea latifolia*

Sweet Pepper-bush
- *Clethra alnifolia* L.
- White Alder family **Clethraceae**

FLOWERING SEASON: July–August. FLOW-ERS: white, many, in numerous slender terminal clusters; about ⅜" (9 mm) wide, with 5 rounded petals; spicy fragrance. PLANT: 3–10' (0.9–3 m) tall; leaves alternate on woody branches, simple, obovate, margin sharply toothed, green. HABITAT: swamps and moist woodlands, mostly near the coast.

Black Nightshade
- *Solanum ptycanthum* Dunal
- Nightshade family **Solanaceae**

FLOWERING SEASON: late July to mid-September. FLOWERS: white with a protruding yellow center, few to several, in loose clusters; about ⁵⁄₁₆" (8 mm) wide, corolla with 5 spreading and some-what recurved, sharply pointed, petal-like lobes. PLANT: 1–2½' (0.3–0.8 m) tall; leaves alternate, simple, ovate, margin usually entire, green; fruit a black berry. HABITAT: waste areas.

Horse-nettle
- *Solanum carolinense* L.
- Nightshade family **Solanaceae**

FLOWERING SEASON: late June–August. FLOWERS: white to bluish white with a protruding yellow center, several, in a loose terminal cluster; about 1" (2.5 cm) wide, corolla shaped like a 5-pointed star. PLANT: about 1–3' (30–90 cm) tall; leaves alternate on a spiny stem, simple, ovate with several deeply cleft, sharply pointed lobes, green. HABITAT: road-sides, meadows, cultivated fields, and waste areas.

Jimsonweed
- *Datura stramonium* L.
- Nightshade family **Solanaceae**

FLOWERING SEASON: August–September. FLOWERS: white, sometimes with a pur-plish center, several, scattered through-out the plant in axils; up to 4" (10 cm) long, corolla bell-shaped with 5 flaring sharp lobes. PLANT: 1–5' (0.3–1.5 m) tall; leaves alternate, simple, ovate, margin with several large, sharp-tipped lobes, green. HABITAT: fields, pastures, and waste areas, sometimes close to the ocean.

Moth-mullein
- *Verbascum blatteria* L.
- Figwort family **Scrophulariaceae**

FLOWERING SEASON: mid-June–August. FLOWERS: yellow or white, several, in a loosely flowered, slender terminal clus-ter; about 1" (2.5 cm) wide, tubular at the base with 5 rounded petal-like lobes. PLANT: 2–6' (0.6–1.8 m) tall; leaves basal and alternate, simple, oblong to lance-shaped with a pointed tip, margin toothed, green. HABITAT: fields and waste areas.

LEAVES ALTERNATE, COMPOUND OR DEEPLY DIVIDED

Multiflora Rose
- *Rosa multiflora* Thunb. ex Murr.
- Rose family **Rosaceae**

FLOWERING SEASON: June. FLOWERS: white with a yellow center, many in axial and terminal clusters; about ¾" (2 cm) wide, with 5 rounded petals; slightly fragrant. PLANT: shrub, 5–10' (1.5–3 m) tall; leaves alternate, pinnately com-pound with 7–9 leaflets; leaflets ovate with a pointed tip, margins toothed, green. HABITAT: old pastures and road-sides.

Horse-nettle / *Solanum carolinense*

Sweet Pepper-bush / *Clethra alnifolia*

Black Nightshade / *Solanum ptycanthum*

Jimsonweed / *Datura stramonium*

Multiflora Rose / *Rosa multiflora*

Moth-mullein / *Verbascum blatteria*

Himalayan Blackberry
- *Rubus bifrons* Vest ex Tratt.
- Rose family **Rosaceae**

FLOWERING SEASON: June. **FLOWERS:** white to rose-tinged, several to many, in terminal clusters; 1–2" (2.5–5 cm) wide, with 5 rounded petals. **PLANT:** shrub, 3–9' (0.9–2.7 m) tall; leaves alternate, palmately compound with 5 leaflets on the lower stem and 3 on the upper stem; leaflets ovate with a pointed tip, margins finely toothed, green above, white to brownish and tomentose below; fruit berry-like, round, nearly black, edible; stem spiny. **HABITAT:** escaped from cultivation in a variety of habitats, but most established in coastal regions. **COMMENTS:** an invasive species with the potential to form troublesome dense stands. Although both blackberries and raspberries are members of the genus *Rubus*, blackberries have palmately compound leaves, ridged stems, conspicuous large-petaled flowers, and berries that are tightly fixed to their stalks. Raspberries (except for purple-flowering raspberry) have pinnately compound leaves, smooth stems, less conspicuous flowers with small easily dislodged and often absent petals, and berries that separate easily from their stalks.

Red Raspberry
- *Rubus idaeus* L.
- Rose family **Rosaceae**

FLOWERING SEASON: June. **FLOWERS:** white to greenish white, several to many, in loosely flowered axial and terminal clusters; about ¼–½" (0.6–1.3 cm) wide, with 5 inconspicuous and easily dislodged erect white petals, surrounded by 5 conspicuous triangular greenish white sepals. **PLANT:** shrub, about 3–6' (0.9–1.8 m) tall; leaves alternate, pinnately compound with 5 leaflets on the lower stem and 3 on the upper stem; leaflets oblong with a pointed tip, margins coarsely and irregularly toothed, green; fruit berry-like, round, bright red, juicy, edible; stem spiny. **HABITAT:** edges of woodlands, woodland trails, and disturbed soils. **COMMENTS:** the black raspberry, *Rubus occidentalis*, has flowers with spreading petals and strongly recurved sepals, and begins blooming within days of the red raspberry's first flowers. The easily dislodged black fruit is edible.

Wineberry
- *Rubus phoenicolasius* Maxim.
- Rose family **Rosaceae**

FLOWERING SEASON: late June–early July. **FLOWERS:** white, several, in loose terminal clusters; about 1¼" (3 cm) wide (including the sepals), with 5 circular white petals that typically remain folded over the stamens and pistil, surrounded by 5 flaring star-shaped sepals. **PLANT:** 3–6' (0.9–1.8 m) tall; leaves alternate, compound with 3 leaflets; leaflets broadly ovate, margins toothed, green; the stems, leaf stalks, and backs of the sepals are densely covered with reddish purple to reddish brown glandular hairs. **HABITAT:** thickets, woodland edges, meadows. **COMMENTS:** the red berries, which ripen in midsummer, are edible.

White Avens
- *Geum canadense* Jacq.
- Rose family **Rosaceae**

FLOWERING SEASON: mid-June to mid-July. **FLOWERS:** white, several in terminal clusters; about ⅝" (1.6 cm) wide, with 5 rounded petals. **PLANT:** 1½–2½' (45–75 cm) tall; leaves basal and alternate; basal leaves with 3 lobes or pinnately compound; stem leaves typically with 3 lobes; leaflets broadly ovate or lance-shaped, margins toothed, green; stem hairy. **HABITAT:** woodlands.

Red Raspberry / *Rubus idaeus*

Himalayan Blackberry / *Rubus bifrons*

White Avens / *Geum canadense*

Wineberry / *Rubus phoenicolasius*

Meadow-sweet, Queen-of-the-meadow

•*Filipendula ulmaria* (L.) Maxim.
•Rose family **Rosaceae**
FLOWERING SEASON: mid-to late July.
FLOWERS: white to off-white, many in a large, showy terminal cluster; about ⅜" (9 mm) wide, with 5 rounded petals; fragrant. PLANT: 2–4' (0.6–1.2 m) tall; leaves alternate, pinnately compound; leaflets ovate to lance-shaped, margins toothed, green. HABITAT: meadows.

Cow-parsnip

•*Heracleum maximum* Bartr.
•Carrot family **Apiaceae**
FLOWERING SEASON: June. FLOWERS: white, many, in rounded, flat-topped terminal clusters 6–12" (15–30 cm) wide; individual flowers tiny, with 5 petals. PLANT: 4–8' (1.2–2.4 m) tall; leaves alternate, compound with 3 leaflets; leaflets broadly ovate, often lobed, margins toothed, green, stem green. HABITAT: moist, usually shaded soils.

Poison Hemlock

•*Conium maculatum* L.
•Carrot family **Apiaceae**
FLOWERING SEASON: mid-June to mid-July. FLOWERS: white, many in numerous rounded, flat-topped, terminal and axial clusters 1–3" (2.5–7.5 cm) wide; individual flowers tiny, with 5 petals. PLANT: 2–5' (0.6–1.5 m) tall; leaves alternate, with 3 large pinnately compound divisions, fern-like; leaflets ovate, margins toothed and deeply divided, green; stem green, usually with purplish markings. HABITAT: waste areas, roadsides, and moist meadows. COMMENTS: *extremely poisonous*.

Water-hemlock, Spotted Cowbane

•*Cicuta maculata* L.
•Carrot family **Apiaceae**
FLOWERING SEASON: July. FLOWERS:

white, many, in rounded, flat-topped terminal clusters 2–4" (5–10 cm) wide; individual flowers tiny, with 5 petals. PLANT: 3–6' (0.9–1.8 m) tall; leaves alternate, pinnately compound with 7–17 leaflets; leaflets lance-shaped with pointed tips, basal leaflets often deeply cleft, margins coarsely toothed, green; stem green with purplish markings. HABITAT: swamps and low grounds. COMMENTS: *extremely poisonous*. Water-parsnip, *Sium suave*, has narrowly lance-shaped, finely toothed leaflets.

Bulb-bearing Water-hemlock

•*Cicuta bulbifera* L.
•Carrot family **Apiaceae**
FLOWERING SEASON: July–August. FLOWERS: white, many, in small, rounded terminal and axial clusters about 1" (2.5 cm) wide; individual flowers with 5 tiny petals. PLANT: 1–3½' (0.3–1.1 m) tall; leaves alternate, divided into several pinnately compound sections; leaflets very narrow, margins sharply toothed, green; bulblet clusters in leaf axils. HABITAT: swamps, edges of ponds and lakes. COMMENTS: *extremely poisonous*.

Queen-Anne's Lace, Wild Carrot

•*Daucus carota* L.
•Carrot family **Apiaceae**
FLOWERING SEASON: July to mid-September. FLOWERS: white, often with a single tiny purple flower in the center of each cluster, many, in rounded, flat-topped terminal clusters 2–4" (5–10 cm) wide; individual flowers tiny, with 5 petals. PLANT: about 1–3' (30–90 cm) tall; leaves alternate, with 1–3 deeply cleft, pinnately arranged divisions, fern-like, margins toothed, green. HABITAT: fields and waste areas. COMMENTS: caraway, *Carum carvi*, also found in sunny areas, is only 1–2' (30–60 cm) tall, has flower clusters 1–2½" (2.5–6.3 cm) wide, and has narrower leaves.

Poison Hemlock / *Conium maculatum*

Bulb-bearing Water-hemlock / *Cicuta bulbifera*

Queen-Anne's Lace, Wild Carrot /
Daucus carota

Cow-parsnip / *Heracleum maximum*

Water-hemlock, Spotted Cowbane / *Cicuta
maculata*

Meadow-sweet, Queen-of-the-meadow /
Filipendula ulmaria

Virginia Waterleaf

- *Hydrophyllum virginianum* L.
- Waterleaf family **Hydrophyllaceae**

FLOWERING SEASON: June. FLOWERS: white to violet, several, in a small, rounded cluster; about 5/16" (8 mm) long, tubular with 5 oblong, petal-like lobes. PLANT: 1–2' (30–60 cm) tall; leaves alternate, pinnately lobed into 5–7 sharply toothed segments, green, often with whitish mottling. HABITAT: woodlands. COMMENTS: broad-leaved waterleaf, *Hydrophyllum canadense*, has similar flowers but broad maple-like leaves.

Yarrow

- *Achillea millefolium* L.
- Aster family **Asteraceae**

FLOWERING SEASON: mid-June to early September. FLOWERHEADS: white, sometimes pinkish, many in a rounded, flat-topped terminal cluster; individual flowerheads about 1/4" (6 mm) wide, rimmed with 4–6 petal-like rays. PLANT: 1–2' (30–61 cm) tall; leaves basal and alternate, finely dissected into pinnatifid segments, lance-shaped, green. HABITAT: fields, roadsides, and waste areas.

LEAVES OPPOSITE OR WHORLED, SIMPLE

Carolina Spring Beauty

- *Claytonia caroliniana* Michx.
- Purslane family **Portulacaceae**

FLOWERING SEASON: mid-April to mid-May. FLOWERS: white to pinkish with darker pink veins, few, in a loose terminal cluster; about 3/4" (1.9 cm) wide, with 5 rounded petals. PLANT: 2–4" (5–10 cm) tall; leaves basal or opposite, simple, broadly lance-shaped, margin entire, green. HABITAT: woodlands. COMMENTS: spring beauty, *Claytonia virginica*, has much narrower leaves.

Bouncing-Bet, Soapwort

- *Saponaria officinalis* L.
- Pink family **Caryophyllaceae**

FLOWERING SEASON: mid-July to early September. FLOWERS: white to pinkish white, many in a dense, rounded terminal cluster; about 1" (2.5 cm) wide, with 5 broad, slightly notched petals. PLANT: 1–2' (30–60 cm) tall; leaves opposite, simple, ovate with a pointed tip, margin entire, green. HABITAT: roadsides, fields, and waste areas.

Mouse-ear Chickweed

- *Cerastium fontanum* Baumg. *emend* Jalas.
- Pink family **Caryophyllaceae**

FLOWERING SEASON: May into September. FLOWERS: white, several, in loose terminal clusters; about 1/4" (6 mm) wide, with 5 petals deeply cleft nearly to the base. PLANT: spreading, 4–12" (10–30 cm) tall; leaves opposite and basal, oblong, hairy, margin entire, green. HABITAT: fields, meadows, and lawns. COMMENTS: common chickweed, *Stellaria media*, has broader, hairless leaves.

White Campion

- *Silene latifolia* Poir.
- Pink family **Caryophyllaceae**

FLOWERING SEASON: June to early August. FLOWERS: white to pinkish white, few in a loose terminal cluster; about 3/4" (1.9 cm) wide, with 5 notched petals and an inflated, hairy, bladder-like base. PLANT: 1–2' (30–60 cm) tall; leaves opposite, simple, broadly lance-shaped, margin entire, green. HABITAT: fields and waste areas.

Carolina Spring Beauty / *Claytonia caroliniana*

White Campion / *Silene latifolia*

Bouncing-Bet, Soapwort / *Saponaria officinalis*

Mouse-ear Chickweed / *Cerastium fontanum*

Virginia Waterleaf / *Hydrophyllum virginianum*

Yarrow / *Achillea millefolium*

Pipsissewa, Prince's Pine
• *Chimaphila umbellata* (L.) Bart.
• Shinleaf family **Pyrolaceae**
FLOWERING SEASON: mid- to late July. **FLOWERS:** white to pinkish white, few to several in a loose terminal cluster; about ½" (1.3 cm) wide, with 5 rounded petals. **PLANT:** 4–10" (10–25 cm) tall; leaves opposite or whorled, simple, broadly lance-shaped, margin toothed, glossy, green, evergreen. **HABITAT:** woodlands.

Spotted Wintergreen
• *Chimaphila maculata* (L.) Pursh
• Shinleaf family **Pyrolaceae**
FLOWERING SEASON: July. **FLOWERS:** white to pinkish, few in a small terminal cluster; about ¾" (1.9 cm) wide, with 5 rounded petals. **PLANT:** 3–10" (7.5–25 cm) tall; leaves opposite to whorled, simple, lance-shaped, margin sharply toothed, dark green with white central veins. **HABITAT:** woodlands.

Miterwort
• *Mitella diphylla* L.
• Saxifrage family **Saxifragaceae**
FLOWERING SEASON: May. **FLOWERS:** white, many on an erect 6–8" (15–20 cm) tall, wand-like cluster; about ⅛" (3 mm) wide, with 5 feathery petals. **PLANT:** 10–18" (25–45 cm) tall; leaves of 2 types: basal leaves heart-shaped and long-stalked; and a pair of opposite, somewhat lance-shaped leaves about one-third of the way up the stem; margins toothed, green. **HABITAT:** rich woodlands.

Blunt-leaf Milkweed
• *Asclepias amplexicaulis* Sm.
• Milkweed family **Asclepiadaceae**
FLOWERING SEASON: June–July. **FLOWERS:** greenish white to pale purple, many, in a rounded terminal cluster; about ⅓" (8.3 mm) long, with 5 deeply recurved petals and a 5-pointed crown-like center. **PLANT:** 2–3' (0.6–0.9 m) tall; leaves opposite, simple, oblong, sessile, margin entire and wavy, green. **HABITAT:** open sandy soils. **COMMENTS:** primarily a species of the coastal plains.

Whorled Milkweed
• *Asclepias verticillata* L.
• Milkweed family **Asclepiadaceae**
FLOWERING SEASON: July–August. **FLOWERS:** white to greenish white, several to many, in loosely flowered terminal and upper axillary clusters; about ¼" (6 mm) long, with 5 deeply recurved pale greenish white petals and a 5-pointed white crown-like center. **PLANT:** 1–2½' (30–75 cm) tall; leaves mostly in whorls of 3–7, simple, long and narrow, margin entire. green. **HABITAT:** dry fields and hillsides.

Hobblebush
• *Viburnum lantanoides* Michx.
• Honeysuckle family **Caprifoliaceae**
FLOWERING SEASON: late April–May. **FLOWERS:** white, many in showy, 3–5" (7.5–12.5 cm) wide flat-topped axial clusters; flowers of 2 types: peripheral flowers large, showy, sterile, about 1" (2.5 cm) wide, corolla with 5 rounded petal-like lobes; central flowers small, fertile, corolla with 5 tiny petal-like lobes. **PLANT:** 2–10' (0.6–3 m) tall; leaves opposite on woody stems, simple, nearly round, margin toothed, green; fruit purplish black. **HABITAT:** woodlands. **COMMENTS:** highbush cranberry, *Viburnum trilobum*, has similar flower clusters but has 3-lobed maple-like leaves and translucent-appearing red fruit.

Pipsissewa, Prince's Pine / *Chimaphila umbellata*

Hobblebush / *Viburnum lantanoides*

Miterwort / *Mitella diphylla*

Spotted Wintergreen / *Chimaphila maculata*

Whorled Milkweed / *Asclepias verticillata*

Blunt-leaf Milkweed / *Asclepias amplexicaulis*

Galinsoga, Quickweed
- *Galinsoga ciliata* (Raf.) Blake
- Aster family **Asteraceae**

FLOWERING SEASON: mid-June through October. FLOWERHEADS: white with a yellow center, many, several in leaf axils; individual flowerheads about ¼" (6 mm) wide, usually rimmed with five 3-toothed petal-like rays. PLANT: 6–19" (15–48 cm) tall; leaves opposite, simple, ovate, margin toothed, green; stems hairy. HABITAT: fields and waste areas.

LEAVES OPPOSITE OR WHORLED, COMPOUND OR DEEPLY DIVIDED

Windflower
- *Anemone quinquefolia* L.
- Crowfoot family **Ranunculaceae**

FLOWERING SEASON: May. FLOWER: white, solitary, terminal, about 1" (2.5 cm) wide, with 5 (4–9) obovate to oval petal-like parts. PLANT: 4–9" (10–22.5 cm) tall; leaves in whorls of 3, palmately divided into 3–5 parts; margins toothed, green. HABITAT: woodlands.

Canada Anemone, Windflower
- *Anemone canadensis* L.
- Crowfoot family **Ranunculaceae**

FLOWERING SEASON: late May to early July. FLOWERS: white, usually 1–3, terminal; about 1¼" (3.1 cm) wide, with 5 large, oblong, petal-like sepals. PLANT: 1–2' (30–60 cm) tall; leaves of 2 types: basal leaves long-stalked and 5-lobed; leaves along upper stem whorled or paired, stalkless and 3-lobed; margins sharply and deeply toothed, green; seedhead rounded. HABITAT: low, moist meadows. COMMENTS: long-headed thimbleweed, *Anemone cylindrica*, has upper leaves with lobes divided to their base and a long, cylindrical seedhead.

Blue Elderberry
- *Sambucus canadensis* L.
- Honeysuckle family **Caprifoliaceae**

FLOWERING SEASON: mid-June to mid-July. FLOWERS: white, many in showy, broad, flat-topped clusters; about ³⁄₁₆" (5 mm) wide, corolla with 5 tiny petal-like lobes. PLANT: 4–10' (1.2–3 m) tall; leaves opposite on woody stems, pinnately compound with 5–7, usually 7, leaflets; leaflets ovate with a pointed tip, margins toothed, green; fruit purple-black, edible. HABITAT: fields and hedgerows. COMMENTS: red elderberry, *Sambucus racemosa*, has cylindrical clusters of dull yellow-white flowers and *poisonous red fruit*; HABITAT woodlands.

FLOWERS SYMMETRICAL, WITH 6 PETALS OR PETAL-LIKE PARTS

LEAVES BASAL, SIMPLE

Wild Leek, Ramp
- *Allium tricoccum* L
- Lily family **Liliaceae**

FLOWERING SEASON: July. FLOWERS: white, many in a nearly spherical terminal cluster on a thin leafless stalk; about ¼" (6 mm) long, perianth with 6 non-spreading parts that give the flower a somewhat tubular appearance. PLANT: 1–2' (30–60 cm) tall; leaves usually 2, basal, simple, oblong to lance-shaped, margin entire, emerging early but withering and disappearing well before flowering, green HABITAT: woodlands. COMMENTS: both the leaves and the bulbs are eagerly sought for their powerful garlic-like flavor.

Blue Elderberry / *Sambucus canadensis*

Canada Anemone, Windflower / *Anemone canadensis*

Galinsoga, Quickweed / *Galinsoga ciliata*

Windflower / *Anemone quinquefolia*

Wild Leek, Ramp / *Allium tricoccum*

Wild Garlic
•*Allium canadense* L.
•Lily family Liliaceae
FLOWERING SEASON: June. FLOWERS: white to pinkish white, 1–3 or more in a terminal cluster with usually 3 sheathing papery bracts beneath; about ¼" (6 mm) wide, perianth with 6 widely spreading, lance-shaped, petal-like parts. PLANT: about 1' (30 cm) tall; leaves basal or nearly so, very long and narrow, slightly flattened, green. HABITAT: fields, moist meadows. COMMENTS: field garlic, *Allium vineale*, is a similar naturalized species with hollow leaves and a single papery bract beneath the flower cluster. Individual flowers have a distinct violet to purplish tinge and a nonspreading perianth, giving the flowers a somewhat tubular appearance.

Yucca
•*Yucca filamentosa* L.
•Agave family Agavaceae
FLOWERING SEASON: July–August. FLOWERS: white, many on a showy branching terminal cluster; about 2" (5 cm) long, perianth with 6 ovate petal-like parts, nodding. PLANT: 2–10' (0.6–3 m) tall; leaves basal, simple, long and narrow, stiff and sharp-tipped, margin entire with curly hair-like filaments, green. HABITAT: sandy soils. COMMENTS: although it is a coastal species, on occasion it has escaped cultivation farther inland. It is common to find a single powder-blue yucca moth in each flower.

LEAVES ALTERNATE, SIMPLE

False Solomon's Seal
•*Maianthemum racemosum* L.
•Lily family Liliaceae
FLOWERING SEASON: late May to mid-June. FLOWERS: white to off-white, many in a branched terminal cluster 1–4" (2.5–10 cm) long; individual flowers about ³⁄₁₆" (5 mm) wide, perianth with 6 oblong petal-like parts. PLANT: 1–3' (30–90 cm) long; leaves alternate, simple, broadly lance-shaped, margin entire, green; fruit a finely speckled pinkish berry. HABITAT: woodlands.

Starry False Solomon's Seal
•*Maianthemum stellatum* L.
•Lily family Liliaceae
FLOWERING SEASON: mid-May to mid-June. FLOWERS: white, several in a short but showy terminal cluster; about ½" (7 mm) wide; perianth with 6 long, narrow, petal-like parts. PLANT: 8–20" (20–50 cm) tall; leaves alternate, simple, lance-shaped with bases somewhat clasping the stem, margin entire, green; fruit a greenish berry with 6 black stripes. HABITAT: moist woodlands, swamps.

Three-leaved Solomon's Seal
•*Maianthemum trifolium* L.
•Lily family Liliaceae
FLOWERING SEASON: June. FLOWERS: white, several in a terminal cluster; about ³⁄₈" (9 mm) wide, perianth with 6 lance-shaped, petal-like parts. PLANT: 2–15" (5–37.5 cm) tall; leaves usually 3, alternate, simple, lance-shaped with base somewhat clasping the stem, margin entire, green; fruit a red berry. HABITAT: bogs, fens, moist woodlands.

White Mandarin
•*Streptopus amplexifolius* (L.) DC.
•Lily family Liliaceae
FLOWERING SEASON: June. FLOWERS: greenish white, several, found singly or occasionally two in axils; about ½" (1.3 cm) long, bell-shaped with 6 sharply pointed deeply recurved tips, pendant. PLANT: 1½–3' (45–90 cm) tall; leaves alternate along an angularly twisted stalk, simple, broadly lance-shaped with a rounded base that clasps the stem, margin entire, green. HABITAT: moist woodlands and wooded swamps.

Yucca / *Yucca filamentosa*

Three-leaved Solomon's Seal / *Maianthemum trifolium*

False Solomon's Seal / *Maianthemum racemosum*

Starry False Solomon's Seal / *Maianthemum stellatum*

Wild Garlic / *Allium canadense*

White Mandarin / *Streptopus amplexifolius*

Wild Cucumber, Wild Balsam-apple, Prickly Cucumber

- *Echinocystis lobata* (Michx.) Tour. and Gray
- Gourd family **Cucurbitaceae**

FLOWERING SEASON: August to early September. FLOWERS: white, many, in erect, slender axial clusters; about ⅝" (1.6 cm) wide, with 6 very narrow petal-like lobes. PLANT: climbing vine, 15–25' (4.5–7.6 m) long; leaves alternate, simple, maple-like with 3–7 lobes; margin minutely toothed, green; fruit about 2" (5 cm) long, ovoid, coated with slender flexible spines. HABITAT: riverbanks, hedgerows, and waste areas.

LEAVES OPPOSITE, DEEPLY LOBED

May-apple

- *Podophyllum peltatum* L.
- Barberry family **Berberidaceae**

FLOWERING SEASON: mid-May to mid-June. FLOWERS: white, solitary, axial; about 2" (5 cm) wide, with usually 6 broad, petal-like sepals and 6–9 tiny oblong petals in the center. PLANT: 1–1½' (30–45 cm) tall; leaves 2 on flowering plants, opposite, appearing terminal, deeply cleft into 5–7 lobes, margin toothed, green. HABITAT: woodlands. COMMENTS: the pulp of ripe fruit is edible.

FLOWERS SYMMETRICAL, WITH 7 OR MORE PETALS OR PETAL-LIKE PARTS

AQUATIC, LEAVES FLOATING

White Water-lily, Fragrant Water-lily

- *Nymphaea odorata* Dryand. ex Ait.
- Waterlily family **Nymphaeaceae**

FLOWERING SEASON: mid-June to mid-August. FLOWERS: white, solitary, terminal; 3–5½" (7.5–13.8 cm) wide, with numerous narrowly oblong petals; fragrant. PLANT: leaves up to 1' (30 cm) long, floating, nearly round with a deeply cleft base, margin entire, green on upper surface, purplish below. HABITAT: aquatic (ponds, lakes, and slowly moving streams).

LEAVES BASAL, LOBED OR DEEPLY DIVIDED

Bloodroot

- *Sanguinaria canadensis* L.
- Poppy family **Papaveraceae**

FLOWERING SEASON: April. FLOWERS: white, solitary, terminal; about 1¼" (3.1 cm) wide, with 8–12 oblong petals. PLANT: 6–14" (15–35 cm) tall; leaves basal, palmate, with 5–9 lobes, margin uneven, green. HABITAT: woodlands. COMMENTS: the damaged root exudes reddish sap that can be used as a dye.

Hepatica

- *Hepatica nobilis* Mill.
- Crowfoot family **Ranunculaceae**

FLOWERING SEASON: April–May. FLOWERS: pinkish, white, or pale blue, several, on individual hairy basal stalks; about ¾" (1.9 cm) wide, with 6–12 lance-shaped, petal-like sepals. PLANT: 4–6" (10–15 cm) tall; leaves basal with long hairy stalks, simple, 3-lobed, usually with an entire margin, green mottled with purple, evergreen. HABITAT: woodlands. COMMENTS: both sharp-lobed and blunt-lobed varieties occur in this region.

May-apple / *Podophyllum peltatum*

Wild Cucumber, Wild Balsam-apple,
Prickly Cucumber / *Echinocystis lobata*

White Water-lily, Fragrant Water-lily /
Nymphaea odorata

Bloodroot / *Sanguinaria canadensis*

Hepatica / *Hepatica nobilis*

LEAVES ALTERNATE, SIMPLE

Ox-eye Daisy
•*Leucanthemum vulgare* Lam.
•Aster family **Asteraceae**
FLOWERING SEASON: late May to late July.
FLOWERHEADS: white with a yellow disc-shaped center, few or solitary, terminal; individual flowerheads 1–2" (2.5–5 cm) wide, rimmed with 20–30 narrow, slightly 2–3 toothed, petal-like rays. PLANT: 1–3' (30–90 cm) tall; leaves alternate, simple, somewhat oblong, margins coarsely and unevenly toothed, green. HABITAT: fields and meadows.

Tall White Aster
•*Aster lanceolatus* Willd.
•Aster family **Asteraceae**
FLOWERING SEASON: September. FLOWERHEADS: white with a yellow center, many, terminal and upper axial; individual flowerheads about ¾" (1.9 cm) wide, rimmed with about 20 petal-like rays. PLANT: 2–8' (0.6–2.4 m) tall; leaves alternate, simple, lance-shaped, margin toothed, green. HABITAT: moist soil.

Flat-topped White Aster
•*Aster umbellatus* Mill.
•Aster family **Asteraceae**
FLOWERING SEASON: August–September. FLOWERHEADS: white with a yellow center, many in a terminal flat-topped cluster; individual flowerheads about ¾" (1.9 cm) wide, rimmed with 10–15 petal-like rays. PLANT: 2–8' (0.6–2.4 m) tall; leaves alternate, simple, lance-shaped, margin entire, green. HABITAT: moist soil.

LEAVES ALTERNATE, DEEPLY DIVIDED OR LOBED

Mayweed, Stinkweed, Dog-fennel
•*Anthemis cotula* L.
•Aster family **Asteraceae**

FLOWERING SEASON: July into September.
FLOWERHEADS: white with a yellow center, several to many in the upper leaf axils; individual flowerheads about 1" (2.5 cm) wide, rimmed with 10–18 minutely 3-toothed, petal-like rays. PLANT: 1–2' (30–61 cm) tall; leaves alternate, deeply cleft into numerous narrow pinnately arranged lobes, green; unpleasantly fragrant if torn. HABITAT: fields, roadsides, and waste areas.

LEAVES WHORLED, SIMPLE

Starflower
•*Trientalis borealis* Raf.
•Primrose family **Primulaceae**
FLOWERING SEASON: mid-May to late June. FLOWERS: white, 1–4, terminal; up to ½" (1.3 cm) wide, with usually 7 petal-like lobes. PLANT: 3–9" (7.5–22.5 cm) tall; leaves in a single whorled cluster, simple, lance-shaped, margin minutely toothed, green. HABITAT: woodlands.

LEAVES WHORLED AND BASAL, COMPOUND

Rue Anemone
•*Thalictrum thalictrioides* (L.) Spach
•Crowfoot family **Ranunculaceae**
FLOWERING SEASON: late April to mid-May. FLOWERS: white or occasionally pinkish, 3 or more, terminal; about ¾" (2 cm) wide, with 5–10 oval petal-like sepals. PLANT: 4–9" (10–22.5 cm) tall; leaves both basal and whorled below flowers, compound; leaflets long-stalked and shallowly 3-lobed, green. HABITAT: woodlands.

Rue Anemone / *Thalictrum thalictrioides*

Ox-eye Daisy / *Leucanthemum vulgare*

Tall White Aster / *Aster lanceolatus*

Starflower / *Trientalis borealis*

Flat-topped White Aster / *Aster umbellatus*

Mayweed, Stinkweed, Dog-fennel / *Anthemis cotula*

FLOWERS NOT RADIALLY SYMMETRICAL; MINUTE, FILAMENTOUS, TUBULAR (OR APPEARING SO) WITH NO PETAL-LIKE LOBES, OR WITH NO OBVIOUS PETAL-LIKE PARTS

LEAVES LACKING

Indian Pipe
•*Monotropa uniflora* L.
•Indian-pipe family **Monotropaceae**
FLOWERING SEASON: July–August. FLOWERS: white to pinkish, solitary, terminal; about ¾" (1.9 cm) long, urn-shaped, with 4-6 petals, nodding. PLANT: 4–10" (10–25 cm) tall; leaves absent; stalk with numerous, tiny leaf-like bracts, white to pinkish, darkening in age. HABITAT: woodlands. COMMENTS: although the urn-shaped flowers appear tubular at first glance, close examination reveals symmetrical floral parts.

LEAVES BASAL, SIMPLE

Sweet White Violet
•*Viola macloskeyi* Lloyd
•Violet family **Violaceae**
FLOWERING SEASON: April–May. FLOWERS: white, sometimes with fine purple veining, several, on individual stalks; up to ½" (1.3 cm) wide, with 5 unequal, rounded petals. PLANT: 1–6" (2.5–15 cm) tall; leaves basal, simple, ovate to nearly round with a heart-shaped base, margin finely toothed, green. HABITAT: moist woodlands.

Lance-leaved Violet
•*Viola lanceolata* L.
•Violet family **Violaceae**
FLOWERING SEASON: May–June. FLOWERS: white, often with a pale-yellow center and purple veining on the lowest petal, several on individual stalks; about ½" (1.3 cm) wide, with 5 unequal, rounded petals. PLANT: 2–6" (5–15 cm) tall; leaves basal, simple, narrowly lance-shaped, margin obscurely toothed, green. HABITAT: woodlands.

Narrow-leaf Plantain, English Plantain
•*Plantago lanceolata* L.
•Plantain family **Plantaginaceae**
FLOWERING SEASON: late May into July. FLOWERS: white, many in a short, ovoid terminal cluster; minute with prominent white-tipped stamens. PLANT: 8–20" (20–50 cm) tall; leaves basal, simple, narrowly lance-shaped, margin entire, green. HABITAT: fields, lawns, and waste areas. COMMENTS: common plantain, *Plantago major*, has broadly ovate leaves and 2–10" (5–25 cm) long, very slender flower clusters.

Pussy's-toes
•*Antennaria neglecta* Green
•Aster family **Asteraceae**
FLOWERING SEASON: May. FLOWERHEADS: white, several in a cluster in the upper leaf axils; individual flowerheads about ¼" (6 mm) wide. PLANT: up to 1' (30 cm) tall; leaves alternate and basal, simple, oblanceolate to narrowly lance-shaped, white, tomentose on the underside, basal leaves with 1 prominent vein, margin entire, green. HABITAT: fields and roadsides. COMMENTS: everlasting, *Antennaria plantaginifolia*, has broader basal leaves with 3 prominent veins.

Narrow-leaf Plantain, English Plantain / *Plantago lanceolata*

Pussy's-toes / *Antennaria neglecta*

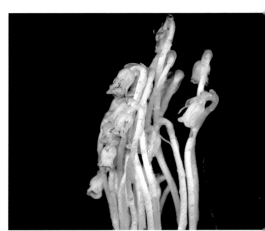

Indian Pipe / *Monotropa uniflora*

Sweet White Violet / *Viola macloskeyi*

Lance-leaved Violet / *Viola lanceolata*

Wild Calla

- *Calla palustris* L.
- Arum family **Araceae**

FLOWERING SEASON: mid-May to early June. **FLOWERS:** greenish white, many on a 1" (2.5 cm) long cylindrical spike framed by a 1–2½" (2.5–6.3 cm) long, broadly lance-shaped, pure white, petal-like spathe; individual flowers minute. **PLANT:** 5–10" (12.5–25 cm) tall; leaves basal, simple, broadly heart-shaped with long stalks, margin entire, green. **HABITAT:** wooded swamps and moist meadows, often in standing water.

Lesser Rattlesnake Plantain

- *Goodyera repens* (L.) R. Br.
- Orchid family **Orchidaceae**

FLOWERING SEASON: July–August. **FLOWERS:** white, 10–20, in a slender terminal cluster; about ⅟₁₆" (1.6 mm) wide, appearing spherical, with 6 unequal petal-like parts. **PLANT:** 5–10" (12.5–25 cm) tall; leaves basal, simple, ovate, margin entire, green usually with wide silvery reticulations. **HABITAT:** moist, mossy pine woodlands. **COMMENTS:** rare. The smallest rattlesnake plantain.

Slender Ladies' Tresses

- *Spiranthes lacera* (Raf.) Raf.
- Orchid family **Orchidaceae**

FLOWERING SEASON: mid-July to late August. **FLOWERS:** white with a greenish center, 5–20 or more loosely spiraled on a slender terminal cluster; about ¼" (5 mm) long, appearing somewhat tubular, with 6 petal-like parts. **PLANT:** 8–24" (20–61 cm) tall; leaves basal, simple, obovate, margin entire, green, may or may not be present during flowering. **HABITAT:** open sandy and often previously disturbed soil. **COMMENTS:** leaf shapes and arrangements are highly variable among the various ladies' tresses. Nodding ladies' tresses, *Spiranthes cernua*, which flowers from late August through September, has ⅜" (9 mm) flowers and a shallowly constricted lip and is common in sunny fens and other moist soils. The physically similar creamy ladies' tresses, *S. ochroleuca*, has white to off-white flowers, is found in drier shadier locations, and blooms from September into October. Wide-leaved ladies' tresses, *S. lucida*, has flowers about ¼" (6 mm) long that are white with a bright-yellow center and blooms in June and July. Two other species of ladies' tresses are primarily coastal in distribution. Little ladies' tresses, *S. tuberosa*, has flowers about ⅛" (3mm) long and blooms in August. Spring ladies' tresses, *S. vernalis*, has flowers about ⁵⁄₁₆" (8 mm) long, has pubescent stems, and blooms from late July through early September.

LEAVES BASAL, COMPOUND OR DEEPLY LOBED

White Clover

- *Trifolium repens* L.
- Bean family **Fabaceae**

FLOWERING SEASON: June to September. **FLOWERS:** off-white, sometimes with a pale pinkish tinge, many, in ¾" (1.9 cm) tall ovoid flowerheads; individual flowers about ¼" (6 mm) long, narrow. **PLANT:** trailing, 4–12" (10–30 cm) long; leaves alternate but appearing basal, compound with 3 leaflets; leaflets obovate, margins finely toothed, green with a pale-green chevron. **HABITAT:** fields, lawns, and waste areas.

Lesser Rattlesnake Plantain / *Goodyera repens*

Wild Calla / *Calla palustris*

White Clover / *Trifolium repens*

Slender Ladies' Tresses / *Spiranthes lacera*

Squirrel-corn
•*Dicentra canadensis* (Goldie) Walp.
•Fumitory family **Fumariaceae**
FLOWERING SEASON: late April to mid-May. FLOWERS: white to greenish white with a pinkish tint, 4–8 in a slender terminal cluster; up to ¾" (1.9 cm) long, heart-shaped and open near the tip, nodding. PLANT: 6–12" (15–30 cm) tall; leaves basal, compound with many long, narrow divisions, green. HABITAT: woodlands.

Dutchman's-breeches
•*Dicentra cucullaria* (L.) Bernh.
•Fumitory family **Fumariaceae**
FLOWERING SEASON: mid-April to mid-May. FLOWERS: white, golden yellow near the tip, several in a slender terminal cluster; about ¾" (1.9 cm) long, V-shaped and open near the tip, nodding. PLANT: 5–10" (12.5–25 cm) tall; leaves basal, compound with many long, narrow divisions, green. HABITAT: woodlands.

LEAVES ALTERNATE, SIMPLE

Lizard's-tail
•*Saururus cernuus* L.
•Lizard's-tail family **Saururaceae**
FLOWERING SEASON: late July–August. FLOWERS: white, many, in slender 4–6" (10–15 cm) long axial clusters; clusters erect with a drooping tip; with usually 6 thread-like stamens and no petal-like parts. PLANT: 2–5' (0.6–1.5 m) tall; leaves alternate, simple, heart-shaped, margin entire, green. HABITAT: swamps and shallow, usually semishaded, water.

Canada Violet
•*Viola canadensis* L.
•Violet family **Violaceae**
FLOWERING SEASON: May through June. FLOWERS: pale violet to nearly white with a yellow center surrounded by fine pur-ple veining, outer surface purple-tinged, several on individual stalks; about ¾" (1.9 cm) wide, with 5 unequal, rounded petals. PLANT: 3–14" (7.5–35 cm) tall; leaves basal and alternate, simple, somewhat heart-shaped, margin toothed, green. HABITAT: woodlands.

Wild Pansy, Field Pansy
•*Viola arvensis* Murr.
•Violet family **Violaceae**
FLOWERING SEASON: May–July. FLOWERS: white with a large yellow basal spot on the lower petal, several, on individual terminal or axillary stalks; about ¼–½" (0.6–13 mm) wide, with 5 unequal, rounded petals. PLANT: 6–10" (15–25 cm) tall; leaves alternate, simple, oval, margin scalloped, surrounded at the base by a pair of large pinnately lobed leaf-like stipules, green. HABITAT: fields, waste areas, disturbed soils.

Swamp Azalea
•*Rhododendron viscosum* (L.) Torrey
•Heath family **Ericaceae**
FLOWERING SEASON: June–early August. FLOWERS: white, several in terminal clusters; about 2" (5 cm) long, tubular with 5 widely flaring lobes, fragrant. PLANT: shrub, 4–8' (1.2–2.4 m) tall; leaves alternate, mostly clustered at the tips of the branches, simple, obovate-oblong, margin entire, green. HABITAT: swamps, moist woodlands.

Dutchman's-breeches / *Dicentra cucullaria*

Squirrel-corn / *Dicentra canadensis*

Canada Violet / *Viola canadensis*

Wild Pansy, Field Pansy / *Viola arvensis*

Lizard's-tail / *Saururus cernuus*

Swamp Azalea / *Rhododendron viscosum*

Lowbush Blueberry

• *Vaccinium angustifolium* Ait.
• Heath family Ericaceae

FLOWERING SEASON: May. FLOWERS: white, few to several in loose terminal clusters; about ³⁄₁₆" (5 mm) long, waxy, tubular and bell-shaped with 5 small teeth. PLANT: shrub, 6–20" (15.5–51 cm) tall, often nearly prostrate; leaves alternate, simple, lance-shaped with a minutely toothed margin, green. HABITAT: dry, rocky, or sandy soil. COMMENTS: produces a delicious fruit.

Velvet-leaf Blueberry

• *Vaccinium myrtilloides* Michx.
• Heath family Ericaceae

FLOWERING SEASON: June. FLOWERS: white, many, in small terminal clusters; nearly ¼" (6 mm) long, waxy, tubular with 5 tiny teeth, nodding. PLANT: shrub, 6–24" (15–60 cm) tall; leaves alternate, simple, oblong with a pointed tip, margin entire, lower surface pubescent, green. HABITAT: moist soils such as fens and swamps. COMMENTS: the fruit is edible.

Fetterbush

• *Leucothoë racemosa* (L.) A. Gray
• Heath family Ericaceae

FLOWERING SEASON: late May to mid-June. FLOWERS: white, many, in 1-sided terminal and axillary clusters; about ¼–⅓" (6–8.3 mm) long, tubular, slightly constricted at the tip with 5 tiny recurved teeth. PLANT: shrub, 4–10' (1.2–3 m) tall; leaves alternate, simple, oblong to ovate, margin minutely toothed, green. HABITAT: swamps, moist thickets. COMMENTS: staggerbush, *Lyonia mariana*, is a coastal shrub with clusters of 4–8, ½" (1.3 cm) tubular white flowers. Although still found on nearby Long Island and points south, there is concern that it may now be extirpated from Connecticut and Rhode Island. Report any sightings to the state conservation department.

Maleberry

• *Lyonia ligustrina* (L.) DC.
• Heath family Ericaceae

FLOWERING SEASON: mid-June to July. FLOWERS: white, many, in terminal clusters; about ¹⁄₁₀" (2.5 mm) long, globular, constricted at the tip, usually with 5 tiny teeth. PLANT: shrub, 2–10' (0.6–3 m) tall; leaves simple, alternate, obovate to oblong, margin minutely toothed or entire, green. HABITAT: swamps and wet soils.

Dwarf Huckleberry

• *Gaylussacia dumosa* (Andr.) Torrey and A. Gray
• Heath family Ericaceae

FLOWERING SEASON: June–July. FLOWERS: white, few to several, in short terminal and axillary clusters; almost ¼" (6 mm) long, tubular to urn-shaped, slightly constricted near the tip with 5 slightly flaring teeth. PLANT: shrub, 1–2' (30–60 cm) tall; leaves alternate, simple, oblong-obovate, margin entire, green. HABITAT: sandy swamps and woodlands.

Fetterbush / *Leucothoë racemosa*

Maleberry / *Lyonia ligustrina*

Staggerbush / *Lyonia mariana*

Velvet-leaf Blueberry / *Vaccinium myrtilloides*

Lowbush Blueberry / *Vaccinium angustifolium*

Dwarf Huckleberry / *Gaylussacia dumosa*

Bearberry, Kinnikinic
•*Arctostaphylos uva-ursi* Spreng.
•Heath family Ericaceae
FLOWERING SEASON: May–June. FLOW-ERS: white to pale pink, few in terminal clusters; about ¼" (5 mm) long, tubular with 5 tiny teeth. PLANT: a trailing or spreading shrub, 6–24" (15–60 cm) long; leaves alternate, simple, oblong to oval, leathery, margin entire, evergreen; fruit a red, mealy, edible berry. HABITAT: dry, sandy, or rocky soil.

Wintergreen
•*Gaultheria procumbens* L.
•Heath family Ericaceae
FLOWERING SEASON: July to early August. FLOWERS: white, usually 1–3; about ¼" (6 mm) long, urn-shaped, somewhat constricted near the tip with 5 slightly flaring teeth, waxy, nodding. PLANT: 2–6" (5–15 cm) tall; leaves alternate, clustered near the top of a woody stem, simple, oval with an obscurely toothed margin, green, glossy, evergreen. HABI-TAT: woodlands, especially under ever-greens. COMMENTS: leaves, pleasantly aromatic when torn, are often used to make a delicious solar tea. The fruit, a bright-red berry, is also edible.

Bog Rosemary
•*Andromeda glaucophylla* Link
•Heath family Ericaceae
FLOWERING SEASON: mid-May to mid-June. FLOWERS: white or pinkish, 3–8 in a drooping terminal cluster; ¼" (6 mm) long, urn-shaped, constricted near the tip, with 5 slightly flaring teeth, waxy. PLANT: shrub, 3–18" (7.5–45 cm) tall; leaves alternate, simple, narrowly lance-shaped with an entire margin, dark green above, downy and white below, evergreen. HABITAT: bogs and fens. COMMENTS: *reportedly poisonous* and not to be confused with culinary rosemary, a member of the mint family.

Cassandra, Leatherleaf
•*Chamaedaphne calyculata* (L.) Moench
•Heath family Ericaceae
FLOWERING SEASON: mid-April to mid-May. FLOWERS: white, several to many in an extended, 1-sided terminal cluster; about ¼" (6 mm) long, tubular with 5 minute teeth, nodding. PLANT: shrub, 2–4' (0.6–1.2 m) tall; leaves alternate, simple, lance-shaped with an obscurely toothed margin, green, evergreen. HABITAT: bogs, fens, and swamps. COM-MENTS: the alternate common name, leatherleaf, refers to the texture of the leaves.

Hedge Bindweed
•*Calystegia sepium* (L.) R. Br.
•Morning-glory family Convolvulaceae
FLOWERING SEASON: late June–August. FLOWERS: pinkish with 5 white stripes or white throughout, several, axial; individual flowers axial, about 2" (5 cm) long and wide, corolla trumpet-shaped. PLANT: trailing and vine-like, 3–10' (0.9–3 m) long; leaves alternate, simple, triangular, margin entire, green. HABITAT: fields and thickets.

Biennial Gaura
•*Gaura biennis* L.
•Evening Primrose family Onagraceae
FLOWERING SEASON: July–August. FLOW-ERS: white turning pink just before wilting, few to several in small terminal clusters; nearly ½" (1.3 cm) wide, with 4 paddle-shaped petals all on the upper half of the flower and 8 conspicuous drooping stamens. PLANT: 2–5' (0.6–1.5 m) tall; leaves alternate, simple, lance-shaped, margin shallowly toothed, green. HABITAT: in dry, sunny soils such as roadsides and fields.

Cassandra, Leatherleaf / *Chamaedaphne calyculata*

Bog Rosemary /*Andromeda glaucophylla*

Wintergreen / *Gaultheria procumbens*

Bearberry, Kinnikinic / *Arctostaphylos uvaursi*

Biennial Gaura / *Gaura biennis*

Hedge Bindweed / *Calystegia sepium*

Silverrod, White Goldenrod
- *Solidago bicolor*
- Aster family Asteraceae

FLOWERING SEASON: September into October. FLOWERHEADS: white, many in a 2–7" (5–17.5 cm) tall slender terminal or shorter upper axial clusters; individual flowers up to ¼" (6 mm) wide, rimmed with usually 6 or 7 tiny petal-like rays. PLANT: 6–48" (0.15–1.2 m) tall; leaves alternate, simple, obovate to oblong, pubescent, margin finely toothed, green. HABITAT: meadows, roadsides, and woodland borders.

Pearly Everlasting
- *Anaphalis margaritacea* (L.) Benth. and Hook. f. ex Clarke
- Aster family Asteraceae

FLOWERING SEASON: August. FLOWER-HEADS: white with a yellow center, many, in dense 2–8" (5–20 cm) wide terminal and upper axial clusters; individual flowerheads about ¼" (6 mm) wide, filamentous, surrounded by numerous pearly, petal-like bracts. PLANT: 1–3' (30–90 cm) tall; leaves alternate, simple, narrowly lance-shaped, pubescent above, woolly below, margin entire, pale green. HABITAT: fields, roadsides, woodland clearings, and waste areas.

Large Solomon's Seal
- *Polygonatum commutatum* (Schultes and Schultes) Dietr.
- Lily family Liliaceae

FLOWERING SEASON: late May to early June. FLOWERS: white with greenish tips, many, in axial clusters of 1 to 8; about ¾" (1.9 cm) long, tubularly bell-shaped with 6 small spreading tips, pendant. PLANT: 1–8' (0.3–2.4 m) long; leaves alternate, simple, broadly lance-shaped, margin entire, green. HABITAT: moist woodlands. COMMENTS: the common name Solomon's seal refers to circular stem scars found on the large root.

Ram's Head Lady's Slipper
- *Cypripedium arietinum* R. Br.
- Orchid family Orchidaceae

FLOWERING SEASON: mid- to late May. FLOWERS: lip white with reddish purple streaking on the lower surface and sides, sepals and petals purplish brown; usually solitary, terminal; lip about ¾" (2 cm) long, pouch-like with a curious spur-like growth on the lower surface. PLANT: 8–12" (20–30 cm) tall; leaves 3–4, alternate, simple, lance-shaped, margin entire, green. HABITAT: damp woods and lakeshores. COMMENTS: *endangered. Do not disturb.*

Lady's Slipper of the Queen
- *Cypripedium reginae* Walt.
- Orchid family Orchidaceae

FLOWERING SEASON: mid-June to the third week of July. FLOWERS: lip white with pinkish rose markings, sepals and petals white; 1 or 2, terminal; lip about 1¾" (4.5 cm) long, pouch-like. PLANT: 12–30" (30–75 cm) tall; leaves 3–7, alternate, simple, broadly ovate, margin entire, green. HABITAT: fens, swamps, moist meadows, and woods. COMMENTS: the tallest lady's slipper found in this region.

Lady's Slipper of the Queen / *Cypripedium reginae*

Pearly Everlasting / *Anaphalis margaritacea*

Silverrod, White Goldenrod / *Solidago bicolor*

Large Solomon's Seal / *Polygonatum commutatum*

Ram's Head Lady's Slipper / *Cypripedium arietinum*

White Fringed Orchid
- *Platanthera blephariglottis* (Willd.) Lindl.
- Orchid family Orchidaceae

FLOWERING SEASON: mid-July through August. FLOWERS: white, 10–20 or more, in a dense terminal cluster; about ⅜–⅝" (9–15 mm) long, with 5 small, petal-like parts and a large, single-lobed heavily fringed lip with a slender basal spur. PLANT: 12–24" (30–61 cm) tall; leaves alternate, simple, narrowly lance-shaped, margin entire, green. HABITAT: sphagnum fens and other open moist areas. COMMENTS: ragged fringed orchid, *Platanthera lacera*, has greenish white flowers with a 3-lobed, very deeply fringed lip.

Tall White Bog Orchid, Bog Candle
- *Platanthera dilatata* (Pursh) Lindl. ex Beck
- Orchid family Orchidaceae

FLOWERING SEASON: mid-June through July. FLOWERS: white, up to 100 in a dense slender terminal cluster; about ⅖–⁷⁄₁₀" (10–18 mm) wide, with 6 spreading, petal-like parts including a lip with a slender basal spur; pleasantly fragrant. PLANT: 12–24" (30–60 cm) or more tall; leaves alternate, simple, narrowly lance-shaped, margin entire, green. HABITAT: fens and moist meadows.

LEAVES ALTERNATE, COMPOUND OR DEEPLY DIVIDED

Tall Meadow-rue
- *Thalictrum pubescens* Pursh
- Crowfoot family Ranunculaceae

FLOWERING SEASON: mid-June through July. FLOWERS: white, many, in showy terminal clusters; about ⁵⁄₁₆" (8 mm) wide, composed of a rounded fluffy mass of thread-like stamens. PLANT: about 3–10' (0.9–3 m) tall; leaves alternate, compound with numerous leaflets;

leaflets somewhat oblong with up to 3 shallow lobes, margin entire, green. HABITAT: open, sunny swamps.

Black Snakeroot
- *Cimicifuga racemosa* (L.) Nutt.
- Crowfoot family Ranunculaceae

FLOWERING SEASON: July. FLOWERS: white, many, in showy slender terminal clusters up to 2 feet long; about ½" (1.3 cm) wide, composed of rounded clusters of thread-like stamens and 4–8 inconspicuous petals; unpleasant fragrance. PLANT: about 3–8' (0.9–2.4 m) tall; leaves alternate, compound with numerous leaflets; leaflets variable, margins sharply and unevenly toothed, green. HABITAT: woodlands.

Allegheny Vine, Climbing Fumitory
- *Adlumia fungosa* (Ait.) Greene ex BSP.
- Fumitory family Fumariaceae

FLOWERING SEASON: June–early August. FLOWERS: off-white to pale greenish purple, many, in axillary drooping clusters; about ½" (1.3 cm) long, somewhat heart-shaped and open near the tip. PLANT: trailing and vine-like; leaves alternate, compound with many distinctly lobed divisions, green. HABITAT: moist wooded areas. COMMENTS: rare.

Canadian Burnet
- *Sanguisorba canadensis* L.
- Rose family Rosaceae

FLOWERING SEASON: August–September. FLOWERS: white, many, in slender 1–6" (2.5–15 cm) cylindrical terminal clusters; about ¼" (6 mm) wide, with 4 prominent filamentous stamens over 4 inconspicuous petal-like parts. PLANT: 1–6' (0.3–1.8 m) tall; leaves alternate, pinnately compound with 7–15 leaflets; leaflets narrowly ovate, margins toothed, green. HABITAT: swamps and moist meadows.

Allegheny Vine, Climbing Fumitory / *Adlumia fungosa*

White Fringed Orchid / *Platanthera blephari-glottis*

Tall White Bog Orchid, Bog Candle / *Platanthera dilatata*

Black Snakeroot / *Cimicifuga racemosa*

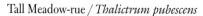

Tall Meadow-rue / *Thalictrum pubescens*

Canadian Burnet / *Sanguisorba canadensis*

White Sweet-clover
•*Melilotus alba* Desr. Ex Lam.
•Bean family **Fabaceae**
FLOWERING SEASON: June–August. FLOW-
ERS: white, many in slender 2–4" (5–
10 cm) long, often 1-sided axial clusters;
about ¼" (6 mm) long, narrowly
pea-like. PLANT: 3–9' (0.9–2.7 m) tall;
leaves alternate, compound with 3
leaflets; leaflets narrowly oblong, margin
toothed, green. HABITAT: fields, roadsides, and waste areas.

Hog Peanut
•*Amphicarpa bracteata* (L.) Rickett
and Stafleu
•Bean family **Fabaceae**
FLOWERING SEASON: August–September.
FLOWERS: pale purplish to white, many,
few to several in long-stalked axillary
clusters; about ½" (1.3 cm) long, pea-
like. PLANT: vine-like, 1–8' (0.3–2.4 m)
long; leaves alternate, compound with 3
leaflets; leaflets broadly ovate, margins
entire, green. HABITAT: moist thickets.

LEAVES OPPOSITE OR WHORLED, SIMPLE

Eyebright
•*Euphrasia stricta* Wolff ex Lehm.
•Figwort family **Scrophulariaceae**
FLOWERING SEASON: August–September.
FLOWERS: white to pinkish white with a
yellow center and purple veining, few to
several in short terminal clusters; about
¼–⅜" (6–9 mm) long, tubular, 2-lipped;
upper lip 2-lobed; lower lip with 3
deeply notched lobes. PLANT: 4–10"
(10–25 cm) tall; leaves opposite, simple,
ovate, margin coarsely toothed, green.
HABITAT: fields and open hillsides.

Bugleweed
•*Lycopus virginicus* L.
•Mint family **Lamiaceae**
FLOWERING SEASON: late July to mid-
September. FLOWERS: white, several to
many in axillary clusters; tiny, tubular,
4-lobed. PLANT: 6–24" (15–61 cm) tall;
leaves opposite on a square stem, simple,
oblong to lance-shaped with a pointed
tip, margin sharply toothed, green.
HABITAT: on wet soil, often near water.

Cow-wheat
•*Melampyrum lineare* Desr.
•Figwort family **Scrophulariaceae**
FLOWERING SEASON: late June into
August. FLOWERS: white with a yellow
lower lip, several, found in pairs in axils;
up to ½" (1.3 cm) long, tubular with 2
short lips. PLANT: 6–18" (15–45 cm)
tall; leaves opposite, simple, narrowly
lance-shaped, margin entire or with 2 or
3 pairs of sharply pointed teeth near the
base, green. HABITAT: woodlands and
thickets.

Turtle-heads
•*Chelone glabra* L.
•Figwort family **Scrophulariaceae**
FLOWERING SEASON: late July to early
September. FLOWERS: white to faintly
pink, several in a terminal cluster;
about 1" (2.5 cm) long, tubular,
2-lipped; upper lip large and hood-
shaped; lower lip 3-lobed. PLANT:
about 1–3' (30–90 cm) tall; leaves
opposite, simple, lance-shaped, margin
toothed, green. HABITAT: swamps, fens,
and along streams.

Hog Peanut / *Amphicarpa bracteata*

White Sweet-clover / *Melilotus alba*

Bugleweed / *Lycopus virginicus*

Eyebright / *Euphrasia stricta*

Cow-wheat / *Melampyrum lineare*

Turtle-heads / *Chelone glabra*

White Beardstongue
- *Penstemon digitalis* Nutt.
- Figwort family **Scrophulariaceae**

FLOWERING SEASON: mid-June to July. FLOWERS: white, several, in a terminal cluster; about 1–1¼" (2.5–3 cm) long, tubular, 2-lipped; upper lip 2-lobed; lower lip 3-lobed. PLANT: 2–5' (0.6–1.5 m) tall; leaves basal and opposite; stem leaves opposite, simple, lance-shaped, margin usually toothed, green. HABITAT: meadows, thickets.

Culver's-root
- *Veronicastrum virginicum* (L.) Farw.
- Figwort family **Scrophulariaceae**

FLOWERING SEASON: August. FLOWERS: white, many, in densely flowered slender 3–9" (7.5–22.5 cm) long terminal clusters; individual flowers about ³⁄₁₆" (5 mm) long, tubular with 4 tiny lobes. PLANT: 2–7' (0.6–2.1 m) tall; leaves whorled in groups of 3–9, simple, lance-shaped, margin sharply toothed, green. HABITAT: moist meadows and woodlands.

Buttonbush
- *Cephalanthus occidentalis* L.
- Madder family **Rubiaceae**

FLOWERING SEASON: mid-July to mid-August. FLOWERS: white, many, in densely flowered 1" (2.5 cm) wide spherical terminal flowerheads; about ⁷⁄₁₆" (1.1 cm) long, tubular with 4 tiny, sharply pointed lobes. PLANT: shrub, 3–12' (0.9–3.6 m) tall; leaves whorled or opposite, simple, ovate with a pointed tip, margin entire, green. HABITAT: swamps and moist meadows.

White Snakeroot
- *Eupatorium rugosum* Houtt.
- Aster family **Asteraceae**

FLOWERING SEASON: mid-July to mid-September. FLOWERHEADS: white, many, in dense, flat-topped terminal clusters; individual flowerheads up to ³⁄₁₆" (5 mm) long, filamentous. PLANT: 1–5' (0.3–1.5 m) tall; leaves opposite, simple, ovate with a pointed tip, margin toothed, green. HABITAT: woodlands.

Boneset
- *Eupatorium perfoliatum* L.
- Aster family **Asteraceae**

FLOWERING SEASON: August to late September. FLOWERHEADS: white, many, in dense terminal clusters; individual flowerheads about ¼" (6 mm) long, filamentous. PLANT: 2–5' (0.6–1.5 m) tall; leaves opposite, simple, joined and perfoliate at the base, lance-shaped, margin toothed, green. HABITAT: wet soil in fields, roadsides, and waste areas.

Buttonbush / *Cephalanthus occidentalis*

White Beardstongue / *Penstemon digitalis*

White Snakeroot / *Eupatorium rugosum*

Culver's-root / *Veronicastrum virginicum*

Boneset / *Eupatorium perfoliatum*

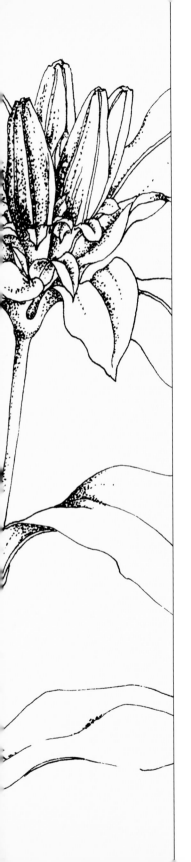

PART TWO

PINK TO RED FLOWERS INCLUDING REDDISH PURPLE

FLOWERS SYMMETRICAL, WITH 3 PETALS OR PETAL-LIKE PARTS

LEAVES WHORLED, SIMPLE

Purple Trillium
•*Trillium erectum* L.
•Lily family **Liliaceae**
FLOWERING SEASON: late April–May. FLOWER: purplish red, solitary, terminal on an erect stalk; about 2½" (6.3 cm) wide, with 3 evenly whorled petals, petals lance-shaped, often slightly recurved. PLANT: 8–16" (20–40 cm) tall; leaves 3, in a whorl at the base of the flower stalk, simple, broadly ovate with a pointed tip, stalkless, margin entire, green. HABITAT: woodlands. COMMENTS: a form with greenish yellow petals is fairly common. Odor unpleasant, like a wet dog.

FLOWERS SYMMETRICAL, WITH 4 PETALS OR PETAL-LIKE PARTS

LEAVES ALTERNATE, SIMPLE

Opium Poppy, Breadseed Poppy
•*Papaver somniferum* L.
•Poppy family **Papaveraceae**
FLOWERING SEASON: July, a few into fall. FLOWERS: variable, white, blue, pink, or crimson, each petal having a large dark spot at the base; several on individual terminal or axillary stalks; 3–4" (7.5–10 cm) wide, with 4 broad petals. PLANT: 1–3' (0.3–0.9 m) tall; leaves alternate, simple, oblong, margin toothed or lobed, pale green. HABITAT: waste areas, disturbed soils. COMMENTS: persisting or spreading from cultivation. Although it is often reported that use of these seeds on breadstuffs causes positive opiate readings on drug screening tests, this may be an urban legend.

Dame's Rocket
•*Hesperis matronalis* L.
•Mustard family **Brassicaceae**
FLOWERING SEASON: late May–June. FLOWERS: white, pink, purplish or variegated, many, in axial and terminal clusters; about ¾" (2 cm) wide, cross-shaped, with 4 rounded petals. PLANT: 2–3' (60–90 cm) tall; leaves alternate, simple, broadly lance-shaped, margin minutely toothed, green; seedpods up to 4" (10 cm) long, slender. HABITAT: fields, roadsides, waste areas, and woodlands.

Honesty
•*Lunaria annua* L.
•Mustard family **Brassicaceae**
FLOWERING SEASON: April–May. FLOWERS: purple, many, in terminal and axillary clusters; ¾–1" (1.9–2.5 cm) wide, with 4 rounded petals. PLANT: 2–4' (0.6–1.2 m) tall; leaves alternate, simple, ovate to somewhat heart-shaped, margin toothed, green; seedpods broadly oval, 1½–2" (3.8–5 cm) long and almost as wide. HABITAT: woodlands, roadsides. COMMENTS: escaped from cultivation.

Daphne
•*Daphne mezereum* L.
•Mezereum family **Thymelaeaceae**
FLOWERING SEASON: mid-April to early May. FLOWERS: rose-purple to occasionally white, many, in clusters of 2–5 along the branches; about ½" (1.3 cm) long, tubular with 4 spreading, petal-like lobes; pleasantly fragrant. PLANT: shrub, 1–4' (0.3–1.2 m) tall; leaves alternate and mostly clustered near branch tips, simple, lance-shaped, margin entire, green. HABITAT: moist woodlands.

Daphne / *Daphne mezereum*

Honesty / *Lunaria annua*

Opium Poppy, Breadseed Poppy / *Papaver somniferum*

Purple Trillium / *Trillium erectum*

Dame's Rocket / *Hesperis matronalis*

Fireweed
• *Epilobium angustifolium* L.
• Evening Primrose family **Onagraceae**
FLOWERING SEASON: mid-July through August. FLOWERS: pinkish purple, many in a slender, pyramid-shaped terminal cluster; about 1" (2.5 cm) wide, with 4 rounded, unequal petals. PLANT: 2–8' (0.6–2.4 m) tall; leaves alternate, simple, lance-shaped, margin entire, green. HABITAT: roadsides, fields, or recently disturbed or burned areas.

Great Hairy Willow-herb
• *Epilobium hirsutum* L.
• Evening Primrose family **Onagraceae**
FLOWERING SEASON: mid-July through August. FLOWERS: rose-purple, several in a terminal cluster; about 1" (2.5 cm) wide, with 4 rounded, distinctly notched petals. PLANT: 2–5' (0.6–1.5 m) tall; leaves alternate, simple, lance-shaped, margin sharply toothed, green. HABITAT: open moist areas and waste areas.

FLOWERS SYMMETRICAL, WITH 5 PETALS OR PETAL-LIKE PARTS

LEAVES BASAL, SIMPLE

Pitcher-plant
• *Sarracenia purpurea* L.
• Pitcher-plant family **Sarraceniaceae**
FLOWERING SEASON: June. FLOWER: purplish red with a yellowish shield-like center, solitary, terminal; about 2" (5 cm) wide, with 5 obovate petals that are narrowed in the middle, nodding. PLANT: 8–24" (20–60 cm) tall; leaves basal, simple, tubular, pitcher-like with downward-pointing stiff hairs on the inner surface, green to red with purple veining. HABITAT: bogs and fens. COMMENTS: a carnivorous plant.

LEAVES ALTERNATE, SIMPLE

Smartweed
• *Polygonum pensylvanicum* L.
• Buckwheat family **Polygonaceae**
FLOWERING SEASON: August–September. FLOWERS: pinkish white to rose, many in densely flowered, cylindrical terminal clusters; minute, with 5 petal-like lobes. PLANT: 1–3' (30–90 cm) tall; leaves alternate, simple, lance-shaped, margin entire, green. HABITAT: fields, cultivated ground, and moist soil. COMMENTS: many species of smartweed, some with arrowhead-shaped leaves and painfully prickly stems, are found in this region.

Hardhack
• *Spiraea tomentosa* L.
• Rose family **Rosaceae**
FLOWERING SEASON: mid-July to mid-August. FLOWERS: rosy pink, many in upright 3–5" (7.5–12.5 cm) tall upper axial and terminal clusters; about $\frac{5}{16}$" (8 mm) wide, with 5 rounded petals. PLANT: shrub, 2–4' (0.6–1.2 m) tall; leaves alternate, simple, oval to oblong, margin coarsely and unevenly toothed, green, woolly on the lower surface. HABITAT: swamps and open moist ground.

Fireweed / *Epilobium angustifolium*

Smartweed / *Polygonum pensylvanicum*

Pitcher-plant / *Sarracenia purpurea*

Great Hairy Willow-herb / *Epilobium hirsutum*

Hardhack / *Spiraea tomentosa*

Purple-flowering Raspberry
•*Rubus odoratus* L.
•Rose family **Rosaceae**
FLOWERING SEASON: June–July. FLOW-ERS: pink to pale purple, few to several in terminal and upper axial clusters; 1–2" (2.5–5 cm) wide, with 5 rounded petals. PLANT: shrub, 2–5' (0.6–1.5 m) tall; leaves alternate, simple, maple-like, 3- to 5-lobed; lobes pointed, margins irregularly toothed, green; upper limbs coated with purplish hairs. HABITAT: along the edges of woods, streams, trails, and roadsides.

LEAVES ALTERNATE, COMPOUND OR DEEPLY DIVIDED

Musk-mallow
•*Malva moschata* L.
•Mallow family **Malvaceae**
FLOWERING SEASON: mid-June through July. FLOWERS: pink or white, often with lavender veins, several, most in terminal clusters; 1½–2" (3.8–5 cm) wide, with 5 broad petals notched at the tip. PLANT: 1–2' (30–60 cm) tall; leaves alternate, with 5 deeply cut and subdivided lobes, green. HABITAT: fields, roadsides, and waste areas.

Sea-beach Rose, Salt-spray Rose
•*Rosa rugosa* Thunb.
•Rose family **Rosaceae**
FLOWERING SEASON: July–August. FLOW-ERS: dark rose-pink to rose-lavender with a yellow center, solitary to several in leaf axials; 2–3" (5–7.5 cm) wide, with 5 rounded petals; fragrant. PLANT: shrub, 2–5' (0.6–1.5 m) tall; leaves alternate, pinnately compound with 5–9 leaflets; leaflets elliptic to oblong, margins toothed, green; stem very spiny and hairy; fruit large, rounded red hips, edible. HABITAT: thickets, sand dunes, and roadsides near the ocean.

Purple Avens, Water Avens
•*Geum rivale* L.
•Rose family **Rosaceae**
FLOWERING SEASON: mid-May to mid-June. FLOWERS: purple, few in a loose terminal cluster; ¾–1" (1.9–2.5 cm) wide, urn-shaped, with 5 rounded petals, nodding. PLANT: about 1–3' (30–90 cm) tall; leaves alternate, pinnately compound; leaflets ovate to lance-shaped, margins toothed, green. HABITAT: swamps and low moist ground.

Purple Cinquefoil, Marsh Cinquefoil
•*Potentilla palustris* (L.) Scop.
•Rose family **Rosaceae**
FLOWERING SEASON: July. FLOWERS: purple, solitary to several, terminal or axillary; ¾–1¼" (1.9–3.1 cm) wide, with 5 tiny petals alternating with 5 larger pointed, petal-like sepals. PLANT: trailing, up to 2' (60 cm) or more long; leaves alternate, pinnately compound; leaflets oblong to oval, margins toothed, green. HABITAT: swamps, fens, and bogs.

LEAVES OPPOSITE OR WHORLED, SIMPLE

Deptford Pink
•*Dianthus armeria* L.
•Pink family **Caryophyllaceae**
FLOWERING SEASON: mid-June to early August. FLOWERS: pink with white dots, one to few in small terminal groups; about ½" (1.3 cm) wide, with 5 elliptical petals that are finely toothed at the tips. PLANT: 6–18" (15–45 cm) tall; leaves opposite, simple, long and narrow, margin entire, green. HABITAT: fields and woodland edges.

Sea-beach Rose, Salt-spray Rose / *Rosa rugosa*

Purple-flowering Raspberry / *Rubus odoratus*

Deptford Pink / *Dianthus armeria*

Purple Avens, Water Avens / *Geum rivale*

Musk-mallow / *Malva moschata*

Purple Cinquefoil, Marsh Cinquefoil / *Potentilla palustris*

Maiden Pink
•*Dianthus deltoides* L.
•Pink family Caryophyllaceae
FLOWERING SEASON: August. FLOWERS: reddish pink with a red-rimmed central eye, solitary to few, terminal; about ½" (1.3 cm) wide, with 5 petals, tips of petals coarsely toothed. PLANT: 6–15" (15–46 cm) tall; leaves opposite, simple, narrowly lance-shaped, margin entire, green. HABITAT: waste areas and meadows.

Ragged-robin
•*Lychnis flos-cuculi* L.
•Pink family Caryophyllaceae
FLOWERING SEASON: late May to mid-June. FLOWERS: pink, several to many, in terminal and upper axial clusters; about ¾" (2 cm) wide, with 5 petals, each petal cleft into 4 long, narrow lobes. PLANT: 1–2' (30–60 cm) tall; leaves basal and opposite, simple, narrowly lance-shaped, margin entire, green. HABITAT: moist fields and meadows.

Marsh St. John's-wort
•*Triadenum virginicum* (L.) Raf.
•Mangosteen family Clusiaceae
FLOWERING SEASON: July–August. FLOWERS: pink with fine purplish veining, several, in terminal and axillary clusters; about ½–⅔" (1.3–1.6 cm) wide, with 5 pointed petals. PLANT: 12–18" (30–45 cm) tall; leaves opposite, simple, ovate to oblong, margin entire, sessile, green. HABITAT: swamps, marshes, fens.

Bog Laurel
•*Kalmia polifolia* Wang.
•Heath family Ericaceae
FLOWERING SEASON: late May to mid-June. FLOWERS: pale pink, several in a loose terminal cluster; about ¾" (2 cm) wide, broadly saucer-shaped, with 5 pointed lobes. PLANT: shrub, 6–24" (15.5–61 cm) tall; leaves opposite or in whorls of 3, simple, narrowly oblong with an entire margin, green, evergreen. HABITAT: bogs and fens.

Sheep Laurel, Lambkill
•*Kalmia angustifolia* L.
•Heath family Ericaceae
FLOWERING SEASON: late May to early July. FLOWERS: dark reddish pink, many in a spherical cluster on the upper portion of the stems; about ½" (1.2 cm) wide, saucer-shaped with 5 shallowly pointed lobes. PLANT: shrub, 6–36" (15–90 cm) tall; leaves opposite or in whorls of 3, simple, narrowly oblong with an entire margin, green, evergreen. HABITAT: in moist soils along woodlands, swamps, and fens. COMMENTS: the alternate common name, lambkill, refers to the *poisonous* nature of this plant.

Scarlet Pimpernel, Poor Man's Weather-glass
•*Anagallis arvensis* L.
•Primrose family Primulaceae
FLOWERING SEASON: July–August. FLOWERS: dull red, several, in terminal and axillary pairs; about ¼" (6 mm) wide, with 5 broad, petal-like lobes. PLANT: usually prostrate with 4–12" (10–30 cm) long branches; leaves simple, opposite, ovate to oval, small, sessile, margin entire, green. HABITAT: open waste areas. COMMENTS: the flower's habit of opening only in sunny weather and closing before a storm gave rise to the alternate common name, poor man's weather-glass.

Scarlet Pimpernel, Poor Man's Weather-glass /
Anagallis arvensis

Ragged-robin / *Lychnis flos-cuculi*

Maiden Pink / *Dianthus deltoides*

Marsh St. John's-wort / *Triadenum virginicum*

Sheep Laurel, Lambkill / *Kalmia angustifolia*

Bog Laurel / *Kalmia polifolia*

Sea-pink, Marsh-pink

• *Sabatia stellaris* Pursh
• Gentian family **Gentianaceae**

FLOWERING SEASON: August. FLOWERS: pink with a yellow center bordered in red, several, terminal; about 1" (2.5 cm) wide, corolla with 5 oval petal-like lobes. PLANT: 6–24" (15–60 cm) tall; leaves opposite, simple, narrow, margin entire, green. HABITAT: salt meadows. COMMENTS: the rare slender marsh-pink, *Sabatia campanulata*, has narrow green sepals the length of the petals, and is found along pond borders.

Common Milkweed

• *Asclepias syriaca* L.
• Milkweed family **Asclepiadaceae**

FLOWERING SEASON: late June to mid-July. FLOWERS: greenish, purple to pinkish white, many in rounded terminal or upper axial clusters; about ⅜" (1 cm) wide, with 5 deeply recurved petals and a 5-pointed crown-like center. PLANT: 3–5' (0.9–1.5 m) tall; leaves opposite, simple, oblong, margin entire, green. HABITAT: fields and waste areas.

Swamp Milkweed

• *Asclepias incarnata* L.
• Milkweed family **Asclepiadaceae**

FLOWERING SEASON: July–August. FLOWERS: red to rose-purple, many in a rounded terminal cluster; about ¼" (6 mm) wide, with 5 deeply recurved petals and a 5-pointed crown-like center. PLANT: 2–4' (0.6–1.2 m) tall; leaves opposite, simple, narrowly lance-shaped, margin entire, green. HABITAT: swamps, moist meadows, and along bodies of water.

Purple Milkweed

• *Asclepias purpurascens* L.
• Milkweed family **Asclepiadaceae**

FLOWERING SEASON: mid-June to July. FLOWERS: deep purple, many, in a round-ed terminal cluster; about ¼" (6 mm) long, with 5 deeply recurved petals and a 5-pointed crown-like center. PLANT: 2–4' (0.6–1.2 m) tall; leaves opposite, simple, ovate to oblong, margin entire, green. HABITAT: dry fields and thickets.

Spreading Dogbane

• *Apocynum androsaemifolium* L.
• Dogbane family **Apocynaceae**

FLOWERING SEASON: late June–July. FLOWERS: pink, several to many, in loose terminal or axial clusters; about 5⁄16" (8 mm) wide, bell-shaped with 5 tooth-like lobes. PLANT: 1–4' (0.3–1.2 m) tall; leaves opposite, simple, oval, margin entire, green. HABITAT: moist fields and meadows. COMMENTS: plant exudes a milky white latex when cut.

Slender Marsh-Pink / *Sabatia campanulata*

Sea-pink, Marsh-pink / *Sabatai stellaris*

Spreading Dogbane / *Apocynum androsaemifolium*

Purple Milkweed / *Asclepias purpurascens*

Common Milkweed / *Asclepias syriaca*

Swamp Milkweed / *Asclepias incarnata*

Summer Phlox
- *Phlox paniculata* L.
- Phlox family **Polemoniaceae**

FLOWERING SEASON: mid-July into September. **FLOWERS:** pink, purple, or white, many in dense, rounded terminal and axial clusters; about 1" (2.5 cm) wide, tubular with 5 nearly round, overlapping, petal-like lobes; fragrant. **PLANT:** 2–5' (0.6–1.5 m) tall; leaves opposite, simple, lance-shaped, margin entire, green. **HABITAT:** meadows and open woodlots. **COMMENTS:** *Phlox maculata* is a shorter plant with smaller flowers and purple-spotted stems.

Seaside Gerardia
- *Agalinis maritima* (Raf.) Raf.
- Figwort family **Scrophulariaceae**

FLOWERING SEASON: August to mid-September. **FLOWERS:** rose-purple, several, terminal; about ¾" (1.9 cm) long, tubular with 5 rounded petal-like lobes. **PLANT:** 4–16" (10–40 cm) tall; leaves opposite, simple, long and narrow, margin entire, green. **HABITAT:** salt marshes. **COMMENTS:** other gerardia species are found inland.

LEAVES OPPOSITE, DEEPLY DIVIDED

Storksbill
- *Erodium circutarium* (L.) L'Hér. ex Ait.
- Geranium family **Geraniaceae**

FLOWERING SEASON: May–October. **FLOWERS:** purple to pink, few to several, in small terminal and axillary clusters; about ⅓" (8.3 mm) wide, with 5 rounded petals. **PLANT:** 6–12" (15–30 cm) tall; leaves basal and opposite, deeply pinnately divided, green. **HABITAT:** woodlands, waste areas, and meadows.

Wild Geranium
- *Geranium maculatum* L.
- Geranium family **Geraniaceae**

FLOWERING SEASON: mid-May to mid-June. **FLOWERS:** rose-purple to occasionally white, 1–3 in loose terminal clusters; about 1¼" (3.1 cm) wide, with 5 rounded petals. **PLANT:** 1–2' (30–60 cm) tall; leaves basal and opposite along the stem, deeply divided into 5 lobes, margin unevenly toothed, green. **HABITAT:** woodlands.

FLOWERS SYMMETRICAL, WITH 6 PETALS OR PETAL-LIKE PARTS

LEAVES ALTERNATE, SIMPLE

Twisted-stalk, Rose Mandarin
- *Streptopus roseus* Michx.
- Lily family **Liliaceae**

FLOWERING SEASON: mid-May to early June. **FLOWERS:** purplish rose, several, found singly or occasionally paired in axils; about ½" (1.3 cm) long, bell-shaped with 6 sharply pointed, often recurved tips, pendant. **PLANT:** 1–2½' (30–75 cm) tall; leaves alternate along an angularly twisted stalk, simple, lance-shaped with a rounded base slightly clasping the stem, margin entire, green. **HABITAT:** moist woodlands. **COMMENTS:** the common name, twisted-stalk, refers to the zigzag appearance of the stalk.

Summer Phlox / *Phlox paniculata*

Wild Geranium / *Geranium maculatum*

Seaside Gerardia / *Agalinis maritima*

Twisted-stalk, Rose Mandarin / *Streptopus roseus*

Storksbill / *Erodium circutarium*

LEAVES OPPOSITE OR WHORLED, SIMPLE

Purple Loosestrife

•*Lythrum salicaria* L.
•Loosestrife family **Lythraceae**
FLOWERING SEASON: July into August.
FLOWERS: purplish pink to reddish purple, many in tall, slender terminal clusters; about ⅝" (1.6 cm) wide, with 6 petals. **PLANT:** 2–4' (0.6–1.2 m) tall; leaves mostly opposite, simple, lance-shaped, margin entire, green. **HABITAT:** swamps, roadsides, and moist soils. **COMMENTS:** an introduced ornamental that has become a serious wetland invader.

~

FLOWERS SYMMETRICAL, WITH 7 OR MORE PETALS OR PETAL-LIKE PARTS

LEAVES ALTERNATE, SIMPLE

Common Fleabane, Philadelphia Fleabane

•*Erigeron philadelphicus* L.
•Aster family **Asteraceae**
FLOWERING SEASON: April–August.
FLOWERHEADS: white to pink with a yellow center, several to numerous, in terminal and upper axial clusters; individual flowerheads about ¾" (2 cm) wide, rimmed with 100–150 narrow petal-like rays. **PLANT:** 1–3' (30–90 cm) tall; leaves alternate, simple, of 2 types: basal and lower leaves spathulate to obovate, somewhat hairy; upper leaves clasping, with a heart-shaped base, somewhat hairy; margin toothed, green; stems hairy. **HABITAT:** fields, woodlands, and waste areas.

New England Aster

•*Aster novae-angliae* L.
•Aster family **Asteraceae**
FLOWERING SEASON: mid-August into October. **FLOWERHEADS:** violet-purple with a yellow center, many, terminal and upper axial, individual flowerheads 1–2" (2.5–5 cm) wide, rimmed with 40–50 petal-like rays. **PLANT:** 2–8' (0.6–2.4 m) tall; leaves alternate, simple, lance-shaped, margin entire, green. **HABITAT:** meadows, roadsides, and along swamps.

LEAVES OPPOSITE, SIMPLE

Plymouth Gentian

•*Sabatia kennedyana* Fern.
•Gentian family **Gentianaceae**
FLOWERING SEASON: mid-July to early September. **FLOWERS:** pink with a yellow center bordered in red, several, terminal; about 1½–2½" (1.3–6.3 cm) wide, corolla with 9–12 petal-like lobes. **PLANT:** 2–3' (0.6–0.9 m) tall; leaves opposite, simple, narrow, margin entire, green. **HABITAT:** wet meadows, along ponds in Massachusetts and Rhode Island. **COMMENTS:** to botanists, this plant symbolizes the fragile ecosystems of the vernal ponds. The large marsh-pink, *Sabatia dodecandra*, a similar southern species with narrower petals, has been reported along the Connecticut coast but may no longer exist in this area. Report any sightings to the state conservation department.

Rose Coreopsis

•*Coreopsis rosea* Nutt.
•Aster family **Asteraceae**
FLOWERING SEASON: July–September.
FLOWERHEADS: pink to rose to nearly white with a yellow center, individual flowerheads ½–1" (1.3–2.5 cm) wide, rimmed with usually 6–8 3-toothed petal-like rays. **PLANT:** 6–24" (15–60 cm) tall; leaves opposite, simple, long and narrow, margin entire, green. **HABITAT:** open swamps, along ponds. **COMMENTS:** found in association with Plymouth gentian in vernal ponds.

~

Purple Loosestrife / *Lythrum salicaria*

Common Fleabane, Philadelphia Fleabane / *Erigeron philadelphicus*

New England Aster / *Aster novae-angliae*

Plymouth Gentian / *Sabatia kennedyana*

Rose Coreopsis / *Coreopsis rosea*

Large Marsh-Pink / *Sabatia dodecandra*

FLOWERS NOT RADIALLY SYMMETRICAL; MINUTE, FILAMENTOUS, TUBULAR WITH NO PETAL-LIKE LOBES, OR WITH NO OBVIOUS PETAL-LIKE PARTS

AQUATIC, LEAVES SUBMERGED

Purple Bladderwort

•*Utricularia purpurea* Walt.
•Bladderwort family **Lentibulariaceae**
FLOWERING SEASON: mid-July into early September. FLOWERS: violet-purple, 1–4, often paired, terminal; about ½" (1.3 cm) long, tubular, 2-lipped; upper lip small and truncate, lower lip 3-lobed. PLANT: aquatic, 1–5" (2.5–12.5 cm) tall; leaves submerged along an underwater stem, filamentous with small globular bladders. HABITAT: ponds, shallow still water.

LEAVES ABSENT OR TYPICALLY LACKING AT FLOWERING

Pinesap, False Beechdrops

•*Monotropa hypopithys* L.
•Indian-pipe family **Monotropaceae**
FLOWERING SEASON: July–August. FLOWERS: white, yellowish or pink, several in a 1-sided terminal cluster; about ½" (1.3 cm) long, appearing tubular, with usually 5 slightly flaring tips, nodding. PLANT: 4–12" (10–30 cm) tall; leaves absent; stalk with numerous tiny leaf-like bracts, white, yellowish, or pink. HABITAT: woodlands.

Arethusa, Dragon's Mouth

•*Arethusa bulbosa* L.
•Orchid family **Orchidaceae**
FLOWERING SEASON: mid- to late June. FLOWERS: rose-magenta, solitary, terminal; about 1¾" (4.5 cm) tall, with 5 somewhat erect, narrowly lance-shaped petals and sepals and a downward curved lip; lip oblong with a wrinkled margin, white with pinkish margins and a tuft of white to yellow hairs. PLANT: 5–10" (13–25 cm) tall; leaf solitary, on the lower stem, simple, long and narrow but not developed at flowering, margin entire, green. HABITAT: sphagnum fens.

LEAVES BASAL, SIMPLE

Moccasin Flower, Pink Lady's Slipper

•*Cypripedium acaule* Ait.
•Orchid family **Orchidaceae**
FLOWERING SEASON: late May–June. FLOWERS: lip pink, sepals and petals light purplish brown; solitary, terminal; lip about 2" (5 cm) long and pouch-like, pendant. PLANT: 6–12" (15–30 cm) tall; leaves 2, basal, simple, broadly oblong, margin entire, green. HABITAT: variable, from dry coniferous or mixed woods to sphagnum fens.

Showy Orchis

•*Galearis spectabilis* (L.) Raf.
•Orchid family **Orchidaceae**
FLOWERING SEASON: late May–late June. FLOWERS: bicolored, pale purplish and white, 3–6 on a slender terminal cluster; about 1" (2.5 cm) tall; 5 sepals and petals, pale purplish, overlapping and hood-like; lip white, pendant, obovate with a prominent spur. PLANT: 4–12" (10–30 cm) tall; leaves 2, basal, simple, obovate, margin entire, green. HABITAT: woodlands.

Calopogon, Grass Pink

•*Calopogon tuberosus* (L.) BSP.
•Orchid family **Orchidaceae**
FLOWERING SEASON: late June–late July. FLOWERS: pink to rose-pink, 3–15 in a slender terminal cluster; about 1¼" (3.1 cm) tall and wide, with 5 oblong to obovate petals and sepals and an erect lip; lip narrow, triangular-tipped, with a conspicuous tuft of white to yellow-

Arethusa, Dragon's Mouth / *Arethusa bulbosa*

Calopogon, Grass Pink / *Calopogon tuberosus*

Purple Bladderwort / *Utricularia purpurea*

Pinesap, False Beechdrops / *Monotropa hypopithys*

Moccasin Flower, Pink Lady's Slipper / *Cypripedium acaule*

Showy Orchis / *Galearis spectabilis*

tipped hairs. **PLANT:** 1–2½" (2.5–6.3 cm) tall; leaf usually solitary, basal, simple, long and narrow, green, margin entire. **HABITAT:** sphagnum fens.

LEAVES MINUTE, OVERLAPPING

Heather
•*Calluna vulgaris* (L.) Hull
•Heath family **Ericaceae**
FLOWERING SEASON: August–early September. **FLOWERS:** pink or white, many, in slender, usually 1-sided terminal clusters; about ¹⁄₁₀" (2.5 mm) wide, urn-shaped or tubular with petal-like lobes. **PLANT:** partially prostrate shrub, 3–15" (7.5–37.5 cm) tall; leaves overlapping, minute, margin entire, green. **HABITAT:** open sandy or rocky soil. **COMMENTS:** persisting or spreading from cultivation. It is common for new foliage to develop above the flower before blooming is complete.

LEAVES ALTERNATE, SIMPLE

Early Azalea
•*Rhododendron prinophyllum* (Small) Millais
•Heath family **Ericaceae**
FLOWERING SEASON: mid-May to mid-June. **FLOWERS:** pale pink, several in a terminal cluster; about 2" (5 cm) long, tubular at the base with 5 unequal and widely flaring lobes; extremely fragrant. **PLANT:** shrub, 2–6' (0.6–1.8 m) tall; leaves alternate, mostly clustered at the tips of the stems, usually emerging with or shortly after the flowers, simple, lance-shaped with an entire margin, green. **HABITAT:** along streams, fens, and mountainous woodlands. **COMMENTS:** frequently attacked by a fungus called *Exobasidium rhododendri*, which transforms some leaves into fleshy, fruit-like structures.

Rhodora
•*Rhododendron canadense* (L.) Torr.
•Heath family **Ericaceae**
FLOWERING SEASON: May–June. **FLOWERS:** magenta, several in showy terminal clusters; about 1" (2.5 cm) long, tubular at the base with 2 extended lobes; upper lobe long and narrow with 3 shallow tips; lower lobe deeply divided. **PLANT:** shrub, 1–3' (30–90 cm) tall; leaves alternate, clustered near the tips of the stems, usually emerging after the flowers, simple, oblong with an entire margin, green. **HABITAT:** fens and damp hillsides.

Black Huckleberry
•*Gaylussacia baccata* (Wang.) Koch
•Heath family **Ericaceae**
FLOWERING SEASON: late May–early July. **FLOWERS:** pink to red, few to several, in short 1-sided clusters; about ¼" (6 mm) long, cylindrical, with 5 tiny teeth. **PLANT:** shrub, 1–3' (30–90 cm) tall; leaves alternate, simple, oval to oblong, margin entire, green; fruit round, very dark blue appearing nearly black, about ⅓" (8.3 mm) wide, edible. **HABITAT:** moist woods, fen edges.

Fringed Polygala, Gaywings
•*Polygala paucifolia* Willd.
•Milkwort family **Polygalaceae**
FLOWERING SEASON: mid-May to early June. **FLOWERS:** rose-purple, 1–4, axial in the upper leaves; about ¾" (1.9 cm) long, appearing tubular with a fringed tip and two petal-like lateral sepals. **PLANT:** 4–7" (10–17.5 cm) tall; leaves alternate, simple, ovate with a pointed tip, margin entire, green. **HABITAT:** woodlands.

Fringed Polygala, Gaywings / *Polygala paucifolia*

Black Huckleberry / *Gaylussacia baccata*

Early Azalea / *Rhododendron prinophyllum*

Heather / *Calluna vulgaris*

Rhodora / *Rhododendron canadense*

Rose Milkwort, Field Milkwort

- *Polygala sanguinea* L.
- Milkwort family **Polygalaceae**

FLOWERING SEASON: July–September. **FLOWERHEADS:** pale rose-purple, sometimes tinged with green, several, terminal, cylindrical to circular, about ½" (1.3 cm) wide and to about 1" (2.5 cm) long, composed of overlapping floral parts. **PLANT:** 6–15" (15–37.5 cm) tall; leaves alternate, simple, long and narrow, margin entire, green. **HABITAT:** meadows.

Cardinal Flower

- *Lobelia cardinalis* L.
- Bluebell family **Campanulaceae**

FLOWERING SEASON: mid-July through August. **FLOWERS:** scarlet, several to many in a showy, slender terminal cluster; about 1¼" (3.1 cm) long, tubular at the base with 5 unequal, spreading petal-like divisions. **PLANT:** 2–4½' (0.6–1.4 m) tall; leaves alternate, simple, lance-shaped, margin toothed, green. **HABITAT:** moist meadows, swamps, and edges of large bodies of water.

Common Burdock

- *Arctium minus* (Hill) Bernh.
- Aster family **Asteraceae**

FLOWERING SEASON: mid-July through August. **FLOWERHEADS:** pink to lavender, several to many in upper leaf axils; individual flowerheads ½–¾" (1.3–1.9 cm) wide, rounded, surrounded by spiny green bracts. **PLANT:** 3–5' (0.9–1.5 m) tall; leaves alternate, simple, broadly ovate, heart-shaped near the base, margin entire, green. **HABITAT:** roadsides and waste areas.

New England Blazing-star

- *Liatris scariosa* (L.) Willd. var. novae-angliae Lunell
- Aster family **Asteraceae**

FLOWERING SEASON: August–September.

FLOWERHEADS: bluish purple, 15–45 along an erect stem, individual flowerheads ½–1" (1.3–2.5 cm) wide, filamentous, base of flowerhead urn-shaped and covered with numerous green bracts. **PLANT:** 1–4' or more (0.3–1.2 m) tall; leaves alternate, simple, long and narrow, margin entire, green. **HABITAT:** dry, open, sandy soils. **COMMENTS:** rare.

New York Ironweed

- *Veronia noveboracensis* (L.) Michx.
- Aster family **Asteraceae**

FLOWERING SEASON: August–September. **FLOWERHEADS:** deep purple, 20–30 in upper, somewhat flat-topped clusters, individual flowerheads about ½" (1.3 cm) wide, filamentous, base of flowerhead urn-shaped and covered with numerous green bracts. **PLANT:** 3–9' (0.9–2.7 m) tall; leaves alternate, simple, lance-shaped, margin toothed, green. **HABITAT:** moist open soils.

Black Knapweed

- *Centaurea nigra* L.
- Aster family **Asteraceae**

FLOWERING SEASON: July–August. **FLOWERHEADS:** rose-purple, solitary to several, terminal, rounded, individual flowerheads about 1" (2.5 cm) wide, base of flower somewhat spherical, covered with deeply fringed, black-tipped bracts. **PLANT:** 1–2' (30–60 cm) tall; leaves alternate and basal, simple, oblong to lance-shaped, margin shallowly toothed to nearly entire, green. **HABITAT:** fields, roadsides, and waste areas. **COMMENTS:** spotted knapweed, *Centaurea maculosa*, has many flowerheads and leaves with narrow, pinnately arranged lobes.

New York Ironweed / *Veronia noveborancensis*

Rose Milkwort, Field Milkwort /
Polygala sanguinea

Cardinal Flower / *Lobelia cardinalis*

Common Burdock / *Arctium minus*

New England Blazing-star / *Liatris
scariosa*

Black Knapweed / *Centaurea nigra*

Saltmarsh Fleabane
- *Pluchea odorata* (L.) Cass.
- Aster family **Asteraceae**

FLOWERING SEASON: August–September. FLOWERS: pinkish to purplish; flowerheads many, in small terminal and upper axial clusters; about ¼" (6 mm) high, cylindrical, filamentous. PLANT: 2–3' (60–90 cm) tall; leaves alternate, simple, ovate to lance-shaped, margin toothed, green. HABITAT: coastal salt marshes. COMMENTS: the dried plant smells like mothballs.

Rose Pogonia, Snake-mouth
- *Pogonia ophioglossoides* (L.) Juss.
- Orchid family **Orchidaceae**

FLOWERING SEASON: late June to mid-July. FLOWER: pink, solitary; about 1¼" (3.1 cm) tall and wide, with 5 lance- to paddle-shaped petals and sepals above the lip; lip oblong with a fringed margin, pink with a central tuft of yellowish hair-like projections. PLANT: 8–15" (20–37.5 cm) tall; leaf usually solitary, on the lower stem, simple, oblong to obovate, margin entire, green. HABITAT: sphagnum fens, moist meadows, and swamps.

Small Purple Fringed Orchid
- *Platanthera psychodes* (L.) Lindl.
- Orchid family **Orchidaceae**

FLOWERING SEASON: late July–late August. FLOWERS: pale purple to lilac or occasionally white, 25–50 or more in a dense terminal cluster; ½–⅝" (1.3–1.6 mm) tall and wide, with 5 rounded petal-like parts and a heavily fringed 3-lobed lip with a long, slender basal spur. PLANT: 1–3' (30–90 cm) tall; leaves alternate, simple, lance-shaped, margin entire, green. HABITAT: sunny, moist meadows and fens. COMMENTS: the large purple-fringed orchid, *Platanthera grandiflora*, has flowers that are about ¾" (1.9 cm) tall and wide in looser clusters, and are often darker in color. This shade-tolerant species begins blooming about one week earlier.

LEAVES ALTERNATE, COMPOUND OR DEEPLY DIVIDED

Red Columbine
- *Aquilegia canadensis* L.
- Crowfoot family **Ranunculaceae**

FLOWERING SEASON: mid-May through June. FLOWERS: scarlet, one to several, terminal; 1–2" (2.5–5 cm) long, with 5 tubular petals displaying yellow coloration near the openings, nodding. PLANT: 1–2' (30–60 cm) tall; leaves alternate, compound with 3–9 leaflets; leaflets wedge-shaped and irregularly lobed, green. HABITAT: variable (for example, rocky woodlands, wet cliffs, and roadsides), frequently near water.

Pink Corydalis
- *Corydalis sempervirens* (L.) Pers.
- Fumitory family **Fumariaceae**

FLOWERING SEASON: late May–June. FLOWERS: pink with a yellow tip, many, in usually 5–10 flowered axial and terminal clusters; about ½–¾" (1.3–2 cm) long, tubular with a rounded spur at the base. PLANT: 1–2' (30–60 cm) tall; leaves basal and alternate, pinnately divided into deeply cleft toothed sections, green. HABITAT: rocky soil.

Crown-vetch
- *Coronilla varia* L.
- Bean family **Fabaceae**

FLOWERING SEASON: June–early August. FLOWERS: bicolored, pink and white, many in dense, clover-like axial clusters about 1" (2.5 cm) wide; individual flowers about ⅜" (9 mm) long, narrowly pea-like. PLANT: prostrate or ascending, up to 2' (60 cm) tall; leaves alternate, pinnately compound with 11–25 leaflets; leaflets oblong, margins entire, green. HABITAT: roadsides and waste areas.

Pink Corydalis / *Corydalis sempervirens*

Rose Pogonia, Snake-mouth / *Pogonia ophioglossoides*

Small Purple Fringed Orchid / *Platanthera psychodes*

Saltmarsh Fleabane / *Pluchea odorata*

Red Columbine / *Aquilegia canadensis*

Crown-vetch / *Coronilla varia*

Beach-pea
•*Lathyrus japonicus* Willd.
•Bean family **Fabaceae**
FLOWERING SEASON: June into August.
FLOWERS: bicolored, pinkish purple to violet and white, many, 6–10 in axial clusters; up to 1" (2.5 cm) long, pea-like. **PLANT**: vine, 1–2' (30–60 cm) long; leaves alternate, pinnately compound with 6–12 leaflets; leaflets oval, margins entire, green. **HABITAT**: ocean beaches, sometimes along large lakes.

Everlasting-pea
•*Lathyrus latifolius* L.
•Bean family **Fabaceae**
FLOWERING SEASON: late June to early August. **FLOWERS**: purplish pink, white or bluish, many, several in dense axial clusters; about 1" (2.5 cm) long, pea-like. **PLANT**: climbing vine, 2–5' (0.6–1.5 m) long; leaves alternate, compound with 2 leaflets and a winged stalk; leaflets oval, margins entire, green. **HABITAT**: roadsides, thickets, and waste areas.

Showy Tick-trefoil
•*Desmodium canadense* (L.) DC.
•Bean family **Fabaceae**
FLOWERING SEASON: mid-July to mid-September. **FLOWERS**: purple to bluish purple, many, in dense terminal and axillary clusters; ½–⅔" (1.3–1.6 cm) long, pea-like. **PLANT**: 2–8' (0.6–2.4 m) tall; leaves alternate, compound with 3 leaflets; leaflets oblong, margins entire, green. **HABITAT**: moist meadows and thickets. **COMMENTS**: the hoary tick-trefoil, *Desmodium canescens*, differs by having a densely pubescent stem and leaf stalks, and smaller ⅕" (5 mm) long flowers.

Bicolor
•*Lespedeza bicolor* Turcz.
•Bean family **Fabaceae**
FLOWERING SEASON: August–September.

FLOWERS: distinctly bicolored, dark purple above, lower parts pale purple, many, several in long-stemmed terminal and axillary clusters; about ½" (1.3 cm) long, pea-like. **PLANT**: 3–10' (0.9–3 m) tall; leaves alternate, compound with 3 leaflets; leaflets oval; margin entire, green. **HABITAT**: moist soils.

Goat's Rue
•*Tephrosia virginiana* (L.) Pers.
•Bean family **Fabaceae**
FLOWERING SEASON: June–July. **FLOWERS**: distinctly bicolored, cream to yellowish wing-like petals above, pink pouch-like center below, many, several in terminal clusters; ½–¾" (1.3–1.9 cm) long, pea-like. **PLANT**: 1–2' (30–60 cm) tall; leaves alternate, pinnately compound with 7–25 leaflets; leaflets narrowly oblong, margins entire, green. **HABITAT**: dry, sandy soils.

Beach-pea / *Lathyrus japonicus*

Everlasting-pea / *Lathyrus latifolius*

Bicolor / *Lespedeza bicolor*

Showy Tick-trefoil / *Desmodium canadense*

Goat's Rue / *Tephrosia virginiana*

Hoary Tick-trefoil / *Desmodium canescens*

Trailing Wild Bean

- *Strophostyles helvula* (L.) Ell.
- Bean family **Fabaceae**

FLOWERING SEASON: July–September. FLOWERS: pale purple to greenish purple, several to many, 3–10 in long-stalked axillary clusters; 1/3–1/2" (8.3–13 mm) long, pea-like. PLANT: usually prostrate and trailing, stem 2–8' (0.6–2.4 m) long; leaves alternate, compound with 3 leaflets; leaflets broadly ovate to somewhat 3-lobed, margins entire, green. HABITAT: coastal meadows and sandy soils.

Red Clover

- *Trifolium pratense* L.
- Bean family **Fabaceae**

FLOWERING SEASON: late May into September. FLOWERS: pinkish red, many in 1" (2.5 cm) tall ovoid flowerheads; individual flowers about 1/2" (1.3 cm) long, narrow. PLANT: 6–24" (15–60 cm) tall; leaves alternate, compound with 3 leaflets; leaflets oval to oblong, margins nearly entire, green with pale-green chevrons. HABITAT: fields and meadows. COMMENTS: rabbit's-foot clover, *Trifolium arvense*, has fuzzy grayish pink flowerheads.

Bull-thistle

- *Cirsium vulgare* (Savi) Tenore
- Aster family **Asteraceae**

FLOWERING SEASON: mid-July through August. FLOWERHEADS: rose-purple, several, terminal and upper axial, individual flowerheads 1 1/2–2" (3.8–5 cm) wide and high, filamentous, base of flowerhead urn-shaped and covered with numerous slender, spiny, yellow-tipped green bracts. PLANT: 2–5' (0.6–1.5 m) tall; leaves alternate, simple, deeply cleft, margin irregular, very sharply toothed and prickly, green. HABITAT: fields, roadsides, and waste areas.

Canada Thistle

- *Cirsium arvense* (L.) Scop.
- Aster family **Asteraceae**

FLOWERING SEASON: late June to July. FLOWERHEADS: lavender to pale rose, many, terminal and upper axial, individual flowerheads about 3/4" (1.9 cm) wide, filamentous, base of flowerhead somewhat spherical and covered with numerous slender, spiny green bracts. PLANT: 1–3' (30–90 cm) tall; leaves alternate, simple, deeply cleft, margin irregular, very sharply toothed and prickly, green. HABITAT: fields and waste areas.

LEAVES OPPOSITE OR WHORLED, SIMPLE OR COMPOUND

Wild Basil

- *Clinopodium vulgare* L.
- Mint family **Lamiaceae**

FLOWERING SEASON: mid-June through September. FLOWERS: pink to purple, several to many in 1" (2.5 cm) wide terminal and axial clusters; about 3/8" (9 mm) long, tubular, 2-lipped; upper lip 3-lobed; lower lip 2-lobed. PLANT: 1–2' (30–60 cm) tall; leaves opposite on a square stem, simple, ovate, margin wavy, green. HABITAT: woodlands.

Bull-thistle / *Cirsium vulgare*

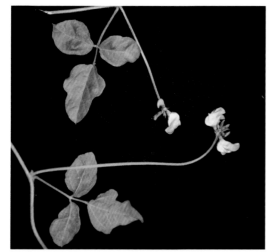

Trailing Wild Bean / *Strophostyles helvula*

Red Clover / *Trifolium pratense*

Canada Thistle / *Cirsium arvense*

Rabbit's-foot Clover / *Trifolium arvense*

Wild Basil / *Clinopodium vulgare*

Peppermint
•*Mentha aquatica x spicata* =
 M. x piperita L.
•Mint family **Lamiaceae**
FLOWERING SEASON: early August into
September. FLOWERS: lavender, many in
whorled, terminal, spike-like clusters;
about ¼" (6 mm) long, tubular, 4-lobed.
PLANT: 1–3' (30–90 cm) tall; leaves
opposite on a square purplish stem,
simple, lance-shaped, margin toothed,
green. HABITAT: moist soils. COMMENTS:
the highly fragrant leaves are the source
of the well-known herbal tea.

Bee-balm
•*Monarda didyma* L.
•Mint family **Lamiaceae**
FLOWERING SEASON: July–August. FLOW-
ERS: scarlet, many in a rounded terminal
cluster; about 1¾" (4.4 cm) long, tubular
with 2 elongated lips; upper lip 2-lobed;
lower lip 3-lobed. PLANT: 2–3' (60–
90 cm) tall; leaves opposite on a square
stem, simple, broadly lance-shaped,
margin toothed, green. HABITAT: moist,
often shaded soils. COMMENTS: a domes-
ticated form is commonly cultivated and
is frequently visited by hummingbirds.

Bergamot
•*Monarda fistulosa* L.
•Mint family **Lamiaceae**
FLOWERING SEASON: mid-July through
August. FLOWERS: lavender, many, in
one or more rounded terminal clusters;
about 1¼" (3.1 cm) long, tubular with 2
elongated lips; upper lip 2-lobed; lower
lip 3-lobed. PLANT: 2–3' (60–90 cm) tall;
leaves opposite on a square stem, simple,
lance-shaped to ovate with a pointed tip,
margin toothed, green. HABITAT: dry
meadows.

Wild Thyme
•*Thymus pulegioides* L.
•Mint family **Lamiaceae**
FLOWERING SEASON: mid-July to early
September. FLOWERS: purple, many in
rounded terminal and axial clusters; tiny,
tubular with 2 lips; upper lip entire;
lower lip 3-lobed. PLANT: prostrate and
creeping, 4–12" (10–30 cm) long; leaves
tiny, opposite on a square stem, simple,
oblong, margin entire, green. HABITAT:
roadsides and meadows. COMMENTS:
thyme makes an excellent culinary
seasoning.

Trumpet-creeper
•*Campsis radicans* (L.) Seem. ex
 Bureau
•Bignonia family **Bignoniaceae**
FLOWERING SEASON: July–August. FLOW-
ERS: scarlet to reddish orange, many, in
terminal clusters of 2–9; about 2½"
(6.3 cm) long, tubular with 5 shallow,
rounded lobes. PLANT: woody vine,
20–40' (6–12 m) long; leaves opposite,
pinnately compound with 7–11 leaflets;
leaflets broadly lance-shaped, margins
toothed, green. HABITAT: woodlands
and thickets.

Trumpet Honeysuckle
•*Lonicera sempervirens* L.
•Honeysuckle family **Caprifoliaceae**
FLOWERING SEASON: June–July. FLOW-
ERS: scarlet, several whorled in a terminal
spike; 1–1½" (2.5–3.8 cm) long, tubular
with 5 small petal-like lobes. PLANT:
vine-like; leaves opposite, upper pairs
joined and perfoliate, simple, oval, margin entire, green. HABITAT: woodlots,
hedgerows, and edges of woodlands.

Trumpet Honeysuckle / *Lonicera sempervirens*

Wild Thyme / *Thymus pulegioides*

Bee-balm / *Monarda didyma*

Trumpet-creeper / *Campsis radicans*

Peppermint / *Mentha aquatica* x *spicata*

Bergamot / *Monarda fistulosa*

Teasel
•*Dipsacus fullonum* L.
•Teasel family **Dipsacaceae**

FLOWERING SEASON: August. FLOWERS: lavender, many, on oval to cylindrical terminal flowerheads; individual flowers about ½" (1.3 cm) long, tubular with 4 tiny rounded lobes. PLANT: 3–6' (0.9–1.8 m) tall; leaves opposite on a spiny stem, simple, oblong to lance-shaped, prickly on the lower central vein, margin entire to bluntly toothed, green. HABITAT: fields and waste areas.

Joe-pye-weed, Red Boneset
•*Eupatorium purpureum* L.
•Aster family **Asteraceae**

FLOWERING SEASON: August to late September. FLOWERHEADS: pink to purplish pink, many, in dense terminal clusters; individual flowerheads about ⁵⁄₁₆" (8 mm) wide, filamentous. PLANT: 3–10' (0.9–3 m) tall; leaves in whorls of 3–6, simple, lance-shaped, margin toothed, green; stem mostly green. HABITAT: moist soil in roadsides, fields, swamps, and woodland edges. COMMENTS: spotted joe-pye-weed, *Eupatorium maculatum*, is a very similar species with flat-topped flower clusters and a purple or purple-spotted stem.

Teasel / *Dipsacus fullonum*

Joe-pye-weed, Red Boneset / *Eupatorium purpureum*

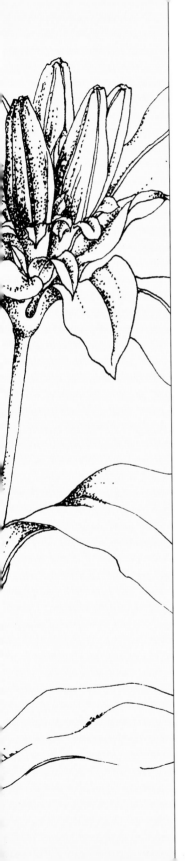

PART THREE

YELLOW TO ORANGE FLOWERS

❧

FLOWERS SYMMETRICAL, WITH 3 PETALS OR PETAL-LIKE PARTS

LEAVES BASAL, SIMPLE

Northern Yellow-eyed Grass
- *Xyris montana* Ries
- Yellow-eyed Grass family **Xyridaceae**

FLOWERING SEASON: July. FLOWERS: yellow, one to few, terminal from a small cone-like head on a very slender stem; about ¼" (6 mm) wide, with 3 rounded, petal-like parts. PLANT: 2–12" (5–30 cm) tall; leaves mostly basal, simple, long and very narrow, margin entire, green. HABITAT: fens and bogs.

Yellow Iris, Yellow Flag
- *Iris pseudacorus* L.
- Iris family **Iridaceae**

FLOWERING SEASON: June–early July. FLOWERS: yellow, several, terminal on an upright stem; about 3¼" (8.1 cm) wide, perianth 6-parted; outer 3 parts obovate with down-turned tips; inner 3 parts smaller, oblong, and nearly erect. PLANT: 1½–3' (45–90 cm) tall; leaves basal, simple, long and narrow, margin entire, bluish green. HABITAT: marshes, wet meadows, and along bodies of water. COMMENTS: because most individuals focus on the 3 prominent down-turned petals and tend not to notice the 3 less conspicuous upright petals, we have placed this wildflower in this section.

FLOWERS SYMMETRICAL, WITH 4 PETALS OR PETAL-LIKE PARTS

LEAVES BASAL, COMPOUND

Wintercress
- *Barbarea vulgaris* R. Br. ex Ait.
- Mustard family **Brassicaceae**

FLOWERING SEASON: mid-May to mid-June. FLOWERS: yellow, several to many in axial and terminal clusters; about 5⁄16" (8 mm) wide, cross-shaped, with 4 oval petals. PLANT: 1–2' (30–60 cm) tall; leaves alternate and basal, upper leaves usually with a few large teeth, basal leaves with a large, oval, toothless terminal division and 1–4 pairs of much smaller lobes along the stalk, green; seedpods about 1" (2.5 cm) long, slender, somewhat spreading. HABITAT: fields and waste areas. COMMENTS: charlock, *Sinapis arvensis*, is 1–2' (30–60 cm) tall and has 5⁄8" (1.6 cm) long seedpods that are constricted around the circular seeds.

LEAVES ALTERNATE, SIMPLE

Witch-hazel
- *Hamamelis virginiana* L.
- Witch-hazel family **Hamamelidaceae**

FLOWERING SEASON: October. FLOWERS: yellow, many, in axillary clusters of 2 to several; about 1" (2.5 cm) wide, with 4 long and very narrow petals. PLANT: shrub, 5–25' (1.5–7.5 m) tall; leaves alternate, simple, oval with an asymmetrical base, margin with large rounded teeth, green. HABITAT: wooded swamps and moist woodlands.

Evening Primrose
- *Oenothera biennis* L.
- Evening Primrose family **Onagraceae**

FLOWERING SEASON: July–September. FLOWERS: yellow, several in a terminal cluster; about 1–2" (2.5–5 cm) wide, with 4 rounded, slightly notched petals. PLANT: 1–9' (0.3–2.7 m) tall; leaves alternate, simple, lance-shaped, margin slightly wavy, green. HABITAT: in dry, sunny soils such as roadsides and fields. COMMENTS: flowers open in early evening and remain open through the following morning.

Northern Yellow-eyed Grass / *Xyris montana*

Wintercress / *Barbarea vulgaris*

Witch-hazel / *Hamamelis virginiana*

Evening Primrose / *Oenothera biennis*

Yellow Iris, Yellow Flag / *Iris pseudacorus*

LEAVES ALTERNATE, COMPOUND OR DEEPLY DIVIDED

Celandine
- *Chelidonium majus* L.
- Poppy family **Papaveraceae**

FLOWERING SEASON: mid-May through June. **FLOWERS:** yellow, few to several, in loose terminal clusters; about ⅝" (1.6 cm) wide, with 4 rounded petals. **PLANT:** 1–2' (30–60 cm) tall; leaves alternate, appearing pinnately compound, margin unevenly bluntly toothed, green. **HABITAT:** moist places and woodlands. **COMMENTS:** the damaged plant exudes bright-yellow, reportedly *poisonous* sap.

Horned Poppy, Sea Poppy
- *Glaucium flavum* Crantz
- Poppy family **Papaveraceae**

FLOWERING SEASON: June–early August. **FLOWERS:** yellow, several, individual flowers terminal on separate stalks, 1–2" (2.5–5 cm) wide, with 4 broad petals. **PLANT:** 2–3' (60–90 cm) tall; leaves alternate, simple, ovate to oblong and deeply lobed, margin toothed, pale green; seed capsule 6–12" (15–30 cm) long, narrow. **HABITAT:** sandy or gravelly beaches. **COMMENTS:** commonly cultivated, found growing wild in only a few coastal locations. Widespread in Europe.

Black Mustard
- *Brassica nigra* (L.) Koch
- Mustard family **Brassicaceae**

FLOWERING SEASON: June–July. **FLOWERS:** yellow, several to many in rounded terminal and axial clusters; about ⅜" (1 cm) wide, with 4 rounded petals. **PLANT:** 2–7' (0.6–2.1 m) tall; leaves alternate, pinnately compound; upper leaflet large and often lobed; lower leaflets few, small; margin toothed, green; seedpods about ½" (1.3 cm) long, tightly appressed to the stem. **HABITAT:** fields and waste areas. **COMMENTS:** the seeds may be used to produce a pungent, hot mustard.

LEAVES OPPOSITE OR WHORLED, SIMPLE

Yellow Bedstraw
- *Galium verum* L.
- Madder family **Rubiaceae**

FLOWERING SEASON: June–July. **FLOWERS:** yellow, many, in densely flowered terminal and axial clusters; tiny, corolla with 4 sharply pointed, petal-like lobes. **PLANT:** 6–30" (15–75 cm) tall; leaves in whorls of 6–8, simple, very narrow, margin entire, green. **HABITAT:** fields and waste areas.

~

FLOWERS SYMMETRICAL, WITH 5 PETALS OR PETAL-LIKE PARTS

LEAVES BASAL, SIMPLE

Marsh Marigold, American Cowslip
- *Caltha palustris* L.
- Crowfoot family **Ranunculaceae**

FLOWERING SEASON: late April–May. **FLOWERS:** yellow, several, in a showy terminal cluster; about 1¼" (3 cm) wide, with 5 large, rounded petal-like sepals. **PLANT:** 1–2' (30–60 cm) tall; leaves mostly basal, simple, heart- to kidney-shaped with a broadly rounded tip, margin entire to slightly scalloped, green. **HABITAT:** swamps and wet meadows.

LEAVES BASAL, COMPOUND

Barren Strawberry, False Strawberry
- *Waldsteinia fragarioides* (Michx.) Tratt.
- Rose family **Rosaceae**

FLOWERING SEASON: late April–May. **FLOWERS:** yellow, several in a loose terminal cluster; about ⁵⁄₁₆" (8 mm) wide, with 5 rounded petals. **PLANT:** creeping, 3–7"

Black Mustard / *Brassica nigra*

Yellow Bedstraw / *Galium verum*

Celandine / *Chelidonium majus*

Horned Poppy, Sea Poppy / *Glaucium flavum*

Barren Strawberry, False Strawberry / *Waldsteinia fragarioides*

Marsh Marigold, American Cowslip / *Caltha palustris*

(7.5–17.5 cm) tall; leaves alternate or mostly basal, compound with 3 leaflets; leaflets obovate, margins toothed, green. HABITAT: woodlands and shaded hillsides.

LEAVES ALTERNATE, SIMPLE

Purslane
•*Portulaca oleracea* L.
•Purslane family **Portulacaceae**
FLOWERING SEASON: July–September. FLOWERS: yellow, several, individual flowers found in the center of axial leaf clusters; up to ¼" (6 mm) wide, with 5 broad petals. PLANT: prostrate; leaves alternate or clustered at the end of 4–10" (10–25 cm) long purple stems, simple, obovate, thick and fleshy, margin entire, green. HABITAT: fields and waste areas.

Velvet-leaf
•*Abutilon theophrasti* Medic.
•Mallow family **Malvaceae**
FLOWERING SEASON: mid-August to late September. FLOWERS: yellow to orange-yellow, 1–3 in the upper axils; about ¾" (1.9 cm) wide, with 5 rounded petals. PLANT: about 3–6' (0.9–1.8 m) tall; leaves alternate, simple, heart-shaped, large, margin entire, green. HABITAT: waste areas and fields, especially with recently disturbed soil. COMMENTS: a nuisance plant of farmers' fields.

Mossy Stonecrop
•*Sedum acre* L.
•Sedum family **Crassulaceae**
FLOWERING SEASON: mid-June to mid-July. FLOWERS: bright yellow, several scattered along spreading stems; about ⅜" (9 mm) wide, with 4–5 lance-shaped petals. PLANT: creeping and spreading, 1–3" (2.5–7.5 cm) tall; leaves alternate, simple, ovate and appearing scale-like, thick and fleshy, margin entire, light

green. HABITAT: on rocks and rocky soil, often wet areas.

Butterfly-weed
•*Asclepias tuberosa* L.
•Milkweed family **Asclepiadaceae**
FLOWERING SEASON: mid-July through August. FLOWERS: orange, many in rounded terminal clusters; about ¼" (6 mm) wide, with 5 deeply recurved petals and a 5-pointed, crown-like center. PLANT: 1–2' (30–60 cm) tall; leaves alternate, simple, narrowly oblong, margin entire, green. HABITAT: dry, often sandy soils.

Clammy Ground-cherry
•*Physalis heterophylla* Nees
•Nightshade family **Solanaceae**
FLOWERING SEASON: July–September. FLOWERS: greenish yellow to yellowish with a brownish to purplish center, several, scattered throughout the plant in axils; about ¾" (2 cm) wide, corolla broadly bell-shaped with 5 petal-like lobes, nodding. PLANT: about 1½–3' (45–90 cm) tall; leaves alternate along hairy branching stems, simple, obovate to broadly heart-shaped, margin toothed, green; fruit an edible spherical berry surrounded by a papery, lantern-like husk. HABITAT: roadsides, waste areas, and previously cultivated fields. COMMENTS: numerous look-alike species occur.

Black Henbane
•*Hyoscyamus niger* L.
•Nightshade family **Solanaceae**
FLOWERING SEASON: June–early September. FLOWERS: greenish yellow with fine purple reticulations, few to several, in loose clusters; 1–2" (2.5–5 cm) wide, corolla with 5 spreading, petal-like lobes. PLANT: 1–2½' (30–76 cm) tall; leaves alternate, simple, ovate to oblong, margin irregularly lobed, green. HABITAT: waste areas and disturbed, sandy soils.

Clammy Ground-cherry / *Physalis heterophylla*

Mossy Stonecrop / *Sedum acre*

Purslane / *Portulaca oleracea*

Black Henbane / *Hyoscyamus niger*

Velvet-leaf / *Abutilon theophrasti*

Butterfly-weed / *Asclepias tuberosa*

Mullein, Velvet Dock, Devil's Tobacco

• *Verbascum thapsus* L.
• Figwort family **Scrophulariaceae**
FLOWERING SEASON: late May–September. FLOWERS: yellow, several to many in an elongated, sometimes branched terminal cluster; up to 1" (2.5 cm) wide, tubular at the base with 5 rounded, petal-like lobes. PLANT: 2–7' (0.6–2.1 m) tall; leaves alternate, simple, oblong, densely pubescent, margin inconspicuously toothed, pale green. HABITAT: fields and waste areas.

LEAVES ALTERNATE, COMPOUND OR DEEPLY DIVIDED

Swamp Buttercup

• *Ranunculus hispidus* Michx.
• Crowfoot family **Ranunculaceae**
FLOWERING SEASON: late April to late May. FLOWERS: bright yellow, several, terminal; 1" (2.5 cm) or more wide, with 5 ovate petals. PLANT: 1–3' (30–90 cm) tall; leaves alternate, divided into 3 segments; leaflets distinctly stalked, margins sharply and unevenly toothed, green. HABITAT: swamps and moist, low ground.

Hooked Crowfoot

• *Ranunculus recurvatus Poir.* ex Lam.
• Crowfoot family **Ranunculaceae**
FLOWERING SEASON: mid-May to mid-July. FLOWERS: light yellow, few, terminal or upper axillary; about ⅓" (8.3 mm) wide, with 5 petals. PLANT: 6–24" (15–60 cm) tall; leaves basal and alternate, deeply 3-lobed, margins toothed, green. HABITAT: woodlands.

Agrimony

• *Agrimonia striata* Michx.
• Rose family **Rosaceae**
FLOWERING SEASON: August into September. FLOWERS: yellow, several to many in slender (usually terminal) clusters; about ³⁄₁₆" (5 mm) wide, with 5 rounded petals. PLANT: 1–5' (0.3–1.5 m) tall; leaves alternate, pinnately compound typically with 5 large leaflets and smaller ones in between; large leaflets oblong to obovate, coarsely toothed, green; smaller leaflets lance-shaped, margins entire, green. HABITAT: dry woodlands.

Common Cinquefoil

• *Potentilla simplex* Michx.
• Rose family **Rosaceae**
FLOWERING SEASON: July. FLOWERS: yellow, few, terminal or in axils; ¼–½" (6–13 mm) wide, with 5 rounded petals. PLANT: trailing, stem 3–24" (7.5–60 cm) long; leaves alternate, palmately compound with 5 leaflets; leaflets oblong to lance-shaped, margins toothed, green; stem hairy. HABITAT: fields, waste areas, and open woods.

Sulfur Cinquefoil, Five-fingers

• *Potentilla recta* L.
• Rose family **Rosaceae**
FLOWERING SEASON: mid-June to mid-August. FLOWERS: sulphur-yellow with an orange center, several to many in a loose terminal cluster; ½–¾" (1.3–1.9 cm) wide, with 5 notched petals. PLANT: 1–2' (30–60 cm) tall; leaves alternate, palmately divided with 5–7 lobes; margin coarsely toothed, somewhat pubescent, green; stem hairy. HABITAT: fields and waste areas.

Hooked Crowfoot / *Ranunculus recurvatus*

Agrimony / *Agrimonia striata*

Mullein, Velvet Dock, Devil's Tobacco / *Verbascum thapsus*

Sulfur Cinquefoil, Five-fingers / *Potentilla recta*

Swamp Buttercup / *Ranunculus hispidus*

Common Cinquefoil / *Potentilla simplex*

Shrubby Cinquefoil
•*Potentilla fruticosa* L.
•Rose family **Rosaceae**
FLOWERING SEASON: late June–July.
FLOWERS: bright yellow, solitary to several, terminal; ¾–1¼" (1.9–3.1 cm) wide, with 5 rounded petals. PLANT: shrub, 6–48" (0.15–1.2 m) tall; leaves alternate, pinnately compound with 5–7 leaflets; leaflets oblong to lance-shaped, silky-pubescent, margins entire or slightly toothed, green. HABITAT: swamps and moist rocky places.

Silvery Cinquefoil
•*Potentilla argentea* L.
•Rose family **Rosaceae**
FLOWERING SEASON: late May–early August. FLOWERS: yellow, few to several, terminal; about ¼" (6 mm) wide, with 5 rounded petals. PLANT: 4–12" (10–30 cm) tall; leaves alternate, palmately compound; leaflets usually 5, oblanceolate, margins toothed, green. HABITAT: meadows.

Wild Senna
•*Senna hebecarpa* (Fern.) Irwin and Barneby
•Mimosa family **Mimosaceae**
FLOWERING SEASON: August. FLOWERS: yellow with brown markings, many, in upper axial clusters; ½–¾" (1.3–1.9 cm) wide, with 5 rounded petals. PLANT: 3–8' (0.9–2.4 m) tall; leaves alternate, pinnately compound with 12–20 leaflets; leaflets oblong, margins entire, green. HABITAT: swamps and moist meadows.

Bigleaf Yellow Avens
•*Geum macrophyllum* Willd.
•Rose family **Rosaceae**
FLOWERING SEASON: June–early August. FLOWERS: yellow, few, terminal; about ½–¾" (1.3–1.9 cm) wide, with 5 rounded petals. PLANT: 1–3' (30–90 cm) tall; leaves basal and alternate; basal leaves pinnately compound; stem leaves typically with 3 deeply divided lobes, margins toothed, green. HABITAT: meadows, roadsides. COMMENTS: the clove-scented roots are the source of a natural red to purple dye.

Yellow Wood-sorrel, Sour Grass
•*Oxalis stricta* L.
•Oxalis family **Oxalidaceae**
FLOWERING SEASON: mid-May through August. FLOWERS: yellow, solitary to several in leaf axils; about ½" (1.3 cm) wide, with 5 nearly round petals. PLANT: 4–12" (10–30 cm) tall; leaves alternate, compound with 3 leaflets; leaflets heart-shaped, margins entire, green, sour-tasting. HABITAT: roadsides, waste areas, fields, and open woodlands.

Wild Parsnip
•*Pastinaca sativa* L.
•Carrot family **Apiaceae**
FLOWERING SEASON: mid-June to mid-July. FLOWERS: yellow, many, in rounded, flat-topped terminal clusters 2–6" (5–15 cm) wide; individual flowers tiny, with 5 petals. PLANT: 2–5' (0.6–1.5 m) tall; leaves alternate, pinnately compound; leaflets ovate, lobed, margin toothed, green. HABITAT: roadsides, fields, and waste areas. COMMENTS: *contact with this plant may cause severe dermatitis in susceptible people.*

Silvery Cinquefoil / *Potentilla argentea*

Bigleaf Yellow Avens / *Geum macrophyllum*

Shrubby Cinquefoil / *Potentilla fruticosa*

Yellow Wood-sorrel, Sour Grass / *Oxalis stricta*

Wild Parsnip / *Pastinaca sativa*

Wild Senna / *Senna hebecarpa*

Golden Alexanders
•*Zizia aurea* (L.) Koch
•Carrot family **Apiaceae**
FLOWERING SEASON: mid-May to mid-June. FLOWERS: yellow, many in a flat-topped terminal cluster about 2½" (6 cm) wide; individual flowers tiny, with 5 petals. PLANT: 1–2½' (30–76 cm) tall; leaves alternate, compound with 3 divisions containing up to 9 leaflets; leaflets ovate to somewhat lance-shaped, margins toothed, green. HABITAT: moist meadows, roadsides, swamps, and edges of open woodlands.

LEAVES OPPOSITE OR WHORLED, SIMPLE

St. John's-wort
•*Hypericum perforatum* L.
•Mangosteen family **Clusiaceae**
FLOWERING SEASON: August. FLOWERS: yellow, several to many in terminal clusters; up to 1" (2.5 cm) wide, with 5 rounded petals with tiny black dots along the margin. PLANT: 1–2' (30–60 cm) tall; leaves opposite, simple, oblong, margin entire, green. HABITAT: fields, roadsides, and waste areas. COMMENTS: there are many species of yellow St. John's-worts in this region. Marsh St. John's-wort, *Triadenum virginicum*, has pinkish flowers in small terminal and axial clusters and is common in fens.

Orange-grass, Pineweed
•*Hypericum gentianoides* (L.) BSP
•Mangosteen family **Clusiaceae**
FLOWERING SEASON: August–September. FLOWERS: yellow, several, terminal or upper axillary, about ¹⁄₁₀" (2.5 mm) wide, with 5 petals. PLANT: 4–20" (10–50 cm) tall; leaves opposite, simple, tiny, margin entire, green. HABITAT: sandy soil.

Beach Heather
•*Hudsonia tomentosa* Nutt.
•Rockrose family **Cistaceae**
FLOWERING SEASON: June–July. FLOWERS: yellow, many, most concentrated along the upper branches, ¼–⅓" (6–8.3 mm) wide, with 5 rounded petals. PLANT: densely branched shrub, 4–8" (10–20 cm) tall; leaves opposite and overlapping, simple, oval to oblong, margin entire, green. HABITAT: sunny, sandy soils along seashores and pine barrens. COMMENTS: the less common *Hudsonia ericoides*, which has needle-like leaves and long-stalked flowers with pointed petals, is also found in this area.

Swamp-candles
•*Lysimachia terrestris* (L.) BSP.
•Primrose family **Primulaceae**
FLOWERING SEASON: late June–July. FLOWERS: yellow with purple markings surrounding the center, many in a tall, slender terminal cluster; about ⅜" (9 mm) wide with 5 narrow petal-like lobes. PLANT: 8–24" (20–60 cm) tall; leaves mostly opposite, simple, lance-shaped, margin entire, green. habitat: swamps and moist areas.

Fringed Loosestrife
•*Lysimachia ciliata* L.
•Primrose family **Primulaceae**
FLOWERING SEASON: mid-July to mid-August. FLOWERS: yellow, several in small axial groups; about ¾" (1.9 cm) wide, with 5 rounded, fringed-tipped, petal-like lobes. PLANT: 1–4' (0.3–1.2 m) tall; leaves opposite or whorled, simple, broadly lance-shaped, margin entire, green. HABITAT: moist meadows and thickets.

Golden Alexanders / *Zizia aurea*

St. John's-wort / *Hypericum perforatum*

Orange-grass, Pineweed / *Hypericum gentianoides*

Beach Heather / *Hudsonia tomentosa*

Swamp-candles / *Lysimachia terrestris*

Fringed Loosestrife / *Lysimachia ciliata*

FLOWERS SYMMETRICAL, WITH 6 PETALS OR PETAL-LIKE PARTS

AQUATIC, LEAVES FLOATING OR JUST ABOVE WATER

Yellow Pond-lily, Spatterdock
•*Nuphar luteum* (L.) Sibth. and Smith
•Waterlily family **Nymphaeaceae**
FLOWERING SEASON: mid-June through August. FLOWERS: yellow, solitary, terminal; 1½–3½" (4–9 cm) wide, with usually 6 oblong petal-like sepals. PLANT: leaves up to 1' (30 cm) long, usually floating, simple, ovate with a deeply heart-shaped base, margin entire, green. HABITAT: aquatic, including ponds, lakes, and slowly moving streams. COMMENTS: some authorities now consider this a complex of several species.

LEAVES BASAL, SIMPLE

Lemon-lily, Yellow Daylily
•*Hemerocallis lilioasphodelus* L.
•Lily family **Liliaceae**
FLOWERING SEASON: mid-May through June. FLOWERS: yellow, several on a tall stem with only 1–3 blooming at a time; about 4" (10 cm) long, large and showy, trumpet-shaped, perianth with 6 flaring and somewhat recurved parts. PLANT: 3–4' (0.9–1.2 m) tall; leaves many, basal, simple, long and narrow, margin entire, green. HABITAT: fields, roadsides. COMMENTS: unlike the orange daylily, *Hemerocallis fulva*, the lemon-lily produces seeds.

Orange Daylily
•*Hemerocallis fulva* (L.) L.
•Lily family **Liliaceae**
FLOWERING SEASON: mid-June through July. FLOWERS: orange, 6–15 on a tall stem with only 1–3 blooming at a time; about 4–5" (10–12.5 cm) long, large and

showy, trumpet-shaped, perianth with 6 flaring and recurved parts. PLANT: 3–6' (0.9–1.8 m) tall; leaves many, basal, simple, long and narrow, margin entire, green. HABITAT: fields and roadsides. COMMENTS: flowers last only one day, hence the common name daylily.

Stargrass
•*Hypoxis hirsuta* (L.) Cov.
•Lily family **Liliaceae**
FLOWERING SEASON: May–July. FLOWERS: yellow, 1–6 in terminal clusters; ½–¾" (1.3–1.9 cm) wide, perianth with 6 long, narrow, petal-like parts. PLANT: 2–6" (5–15 cm) tall; leaves basal, simple, long and narrow, margin entire, green. HABITAT: open and often semishaded areas.

Troutlily, Dog-tooth Violet
•*Erythronium americanum* Ker
•Lily family **Liliaceae**
FLOWERING SEASON: late April to mid-May. FLOWER: yellow, solitary, terminal; about 1¼" (3.1 cm) long, perianth with 6 lance-shaped spreading to somewhat recurved parts. PLANT: 6–12" (15–30 cm) tall; leaves 2, basal, simple, lance-shaped, margin entire, fleshy, green, often with purplish or brownish mottling. HABITAT: woodlands.

Clintonia, Woodlily
•*Clintonia borealis* (Ait.) Raf.
•Lily family **Liliaceae**
FLOWERING SEASON: late May–June. FLOWERS: yellow to greenish yellow, 3–6 in a terminal cluster; about ¾" (1.9 cm) long, perianth with 6 long, narrow petal-like parts, usually drooping. PLANT: 6–15" (15.5–37.5 cm) tall; leaves usually 3, basal, simple, oval, margin entire, green. HABITAT: woodlands.

Yellow Pond-lily, Spatterdock / *Nuphar luteum*

Lemon-lily, Yellow Daylily / *Hemerocallis lilioasphodelus*

Orange Daylily / *Hemerocallis fulva*

Clintonia, Woodlily / *Clintonia borealis*

Troutlily, Dog-tooth Violet / *Erythronium americanum*

Stargrass / *Hypoxis hirsuta*

LEAVES ALTERNATE, SIMPLE

Tiger Lily
• *Lilium lancifolium* Thunb.
• Lily family **Liliaceae**

FLOWERING SEASON: mid-July to mid-August. FLOWERS: orange-red, conspicuously purple-spotted inside, 5–25 flowers in a terminal cluster; about 3¼" (8.1 cm) wide, perianth with 6 large, spreading, and deeply recurved petal-like parts, stamens fully protruding, nodding. PLANT: 2–5' (0.6–1.5 m) tall; leaves alternate, simple, lance-shaped, margin entire, green; blackish bulblets in the upper axils. HABITAT: fields, hedgerows, and roadsides.

Wild-oats
• *Uvularia sessilifolia* L.
• Lily family **Liliaceae**

FLOWERING SEASON: mid- to late May. FLOWER: greenish yellow, solitary, axial; about 1" (2.5 cm) long, perianth with 6 long, narrow, petal-like parts, nodding. PLANT: 10–12" (25–30 cm) tall; leaves alternate along a forking stem, simple, lance-shaped, margin entire, green. HABITAT: woodlands.

Bellwort
• *Uvularia grandiflora* Sm.
• Lily family **Liliaceae**

FLOWERING SEASON: mid-April to mid-May. FLOWER: yellow, usually solitary and terminal; about 1¼" (3.1 cm) long, perianth with 6 long, narrow, petal-like parts, smooth or slightly granular within, nodding. PLANT: 6–20" (15–50 cm) tall; leaves alternate on a forking stem, simple, oblong to oval, penetrated by the stem, margin entire, lower surface pubescent during flowering season, green. HABITAT: woodlands.

LEAVES ALTERNATE, COMPOUND OR DEEPLY LOBED

Globeflower
• *Trollius laxus* Salisb.
• Crowfoot family **Ranunculaceae**

FLOWERING SEASON: mid-April into May. FLOWER: pale greenish yellow, usually solitary, terminal, about 1½" (3.8 cm) wide, with 5–7 oval petal-like sepals. PLANT: 6–18" (15–45 cm) tall; leaves alternate, compound with 5–7 deeply cut lobes, lower leaves long-stalked, margins sharply and deeply toothed, green. HABITAT: swamps and wet meadows.

LEAVES OPPOSITE OR WHORLED, SIMPLE

Common Barberry
• *Berberis vulgaris* L.
• Barberry family **Berberidaceae**

FLOWERING SEASON: mid-May to mid-June. FLOWERS: yellow, several to many in pendant, slender axial clusters; about ⁵⁄₁₆" (8 mm) wide, with 6 rounded petals. PLANT: shrub, 6–8' (1.8–2.4 m) tall; leaves opposite or whorled, simple, paddle-shaped, margin sharply toothed, green. HABITAT: thickets, pastures, and hedgerows. COMMENTS: the scarlet oblong berries are used in tart beverages.

Indian Cucumber-root
• *Medeola virginiana* L.
• Lily family **Liliaceae**

FLOWERING SEASON: June to early July. FLOWERS: greenish yellow, 2–9 in a drooping terminal cluster; about ¾" (2 cm) wide, perianth with 6 petal-like parts. PLANT: 1–2½' (30–75 cm) tall; leaves in 2 whorls; leaves of lower whorl large and about 6 in number, leaves of upper whorl smaller, fewer, terminal; simple, lance-shaped, margin entire, green. HABITAT: woodlands.

Bellwort / *Uvularia grandiflora*

Wild-oats / *Uvularia sessilifolia*

Globeflower / *Trollius laxus*

Indian Cucumber-root / *Medeola virginiana*

Tiger Lily / *Lilium lancifolium*

Common Barberry / *Berberis vulgaris*

Woodlily
- *Lilium philadelphicum* L.
- Lily family Liliaceae

FLOWERING SEASON: late June to early July. **FLOWER:** reddish orange, purple-spotted inside, usually solitary or sometimes 2, terminal; about 3½" (8.8 cm) wide, perianth with 6 spreading, petal-like parts, flower facing upward. **PLANT:** 1–3' (30–90 cm) tall; leaves whorled, simple, lance-shaped, margin entire, green. **HABITAT:** woods and thickets.

Canada Lily
- *Lilium canadense* L.
- Lily family Liliaceae

FLOWERING SEASON: late June to mid-July. **FLOWERS:** yellow, occasionally red, with numerous spots inside, 1–16 in showy terminal clusters; about 3¾" (9.4 cm) wide, perianth with 6 large, spreading, and somewhat recurved petal-like parts, thickened tips of stamens protruding from flowers, nodding. **PLANT:** 2–5' (0.6–1.5 m) tall; leaves whorled, simple, lance-shaped, margin entire, green. **HABITAT:** swamps, moist meadows, and fields.

Turk's-cap Lily
- *Lilium superbum* L.
- Lily family Liliaceae

FLOWERING SEASON: July. **FLOWERS:** orange, orange-yellow, or occasionally red, purple-spotted inside, 3–40 in showy terminal clusters; about 3" (7.5 cm) wide, perianth with 6 large, spreading, and deeply recurved petal-like parts, nearly all of the stamens protruding from flowers, nodding. **PLANT:** 3–8' (0.9–2.4 m) tall; leaves whorled, simple, lance-shaped, margin entire, green. **HABITAT:** meadows and open moist areas.

FLOWERS SYMMETRICAL, WITH 7 OR MORE PETALS OR PETAL-LIKE PARTS

LACKING TYPICAL LEAVES

Prickly Pear
- *Opuntia humifusa* (Raf.) Raf.
- Cactus family Cactaceae

FLOWERING SEASON: July. **FLOWERS:** yellow, several, arising from pads; 2½–3½" (6.3–8.8 cm) wide, with numerous broad petals. **PLANT:** usually prostrate; pads obovate to oval, thick and fleshy, covered with clusters of needle-like spines, green. **HABITAT:** in sandy soil. **COMMENTS:** New England's only cactus species.

AQUATIC, LEAVES SUSPENDED ABOVE WATER

Yellow Lotus
- *Nelumbo lutea* (Willd.) Pers.
- Lotus family Nelumbonaceae

FLOWERING SEASON: mid-July to mid-August. **FLOWERS:** pale yellow, solitary, rising above the water on a single stalk; 4–10" (10–25 cm) wide, with many obovate petals. **PLANT:** leaves 1–2' (30–60 cm) wide, usually held above water or occasionally floating, simple, nearly round and somewhat funnel-shaped, margin entire, green. **HABITAT:** aquatic (lakes and slowly moving rivers). **COMMENTS:** the dried seedhead, which resembles an old-fashioned showerhead, is commonly used in dried flower arrangements.

Turk's-cap Lily / *Lilium superbum*

Prickly Pear / *Opuntia humifusa*

Woodlily / *Lilium philadelphicum*

Yellow Lotus / *Nelumbo lutea*

Canada Lily / *Lilium canadense*

LEAVES BASAL, SIMPLE

Dandelion
- *Taraxacum officinale* Weber ex Wiggers
- Aster family **Asteraceae**

FLOWERING SEASON: late April to early June; a few into fall. FLOWERHEADS: yellow, 1 to few on terminal stalks; individual flowerheads about 1½" (3.8 cm) wide, rimmed with many oblong, minutely 5-toothed, petal-like rays. PLANT: 2–18" (5–45 cm) tall; leaves basal, simple, oblong to paddle-shaped, margin unevenly and coarsely toothed, green. HABITAT: fields, lawns, and waste areas.

Cat's Ear
- *Hypochaeris radicata* L.
- Aster family **Asteraceae**

FLOWERING SEASON: mid-July to September. FLOWERHEADS: yellow, several in small terminal clusters; individual flowerheads about 1" (2.5 cm) wide, rimmed with many rectangular, minutely 5-toothed, petal-like rays. PLANT: 1–2' (30–60 cm) tall; leaves basal, simple, oblong to paddle-shaped, margin unevenly and coarsely toothed, pubescent, green. HABITAT: waste areas and fields.

Coltsfoot
- *Tussilago farfara* L.
- Aster family **Asteraceae**

FLOWERING SEASON: April–May. FLOWERHEADS: yellow, few, each terminal on an individual scaly 3–18" (7.5–45 cm) tall stem; individual flowerheads about 1" (2.5 cm) wide, rimmed with many narrow, petal-like rays, blooming before the leaves emerge. LEAVES: basal, simple, nearly round with very shallow angularly sided lobes, margin toothed, green, pubescent underneath. HABITAT: moist soil, meadows, and roadsides.

LEAVES ALTERNATE, SIMPLE

Elecampane
- *Inula helenium* L.
- Aster family **Asteraceae**

FLOWERING SEASON: mid-July to mid-August. FLOWERHEADS: yellow, several, terminal; individual flowerheads 2–4" (5–10 cm) wide, rimmed with many very narrow, minutely 3-toothed, petal-like rays. PLANT: 2–6' (0.6–1.8 m) tall; leaves alternate and basal, simple, broadly lance-shaped, rough textured, margin toothed, green. HABITAT: moist meadows.

Yellow Goat's-beard
- *Tragopogon pratensis* L.
- Aster family **Asteraceae**

FLOWERING SEASON: mid-May to late June. FLOWERHEAD: yellow, solitary, terminal, 1½–2½" (3.8–6.3 cm) wide, rimmed with many oblong, minutely 5-toothed, petal-like rays. PLANT: 15–36" (37.5–90 cm) tall; leaves basal and alternate, simple, long and narrow, margin entire, green. HABITAT: fields and waste areas. COMMENTS: salsify, *Tragopogon porrifolius*, is a very similar plant with purplish flowerheads.

Black-eyed Susan
- *Rudbeckia hirta* L.
- Aster family **Asteraceae**

FLOWERING SEASON: July–August. FLOWERHEADS: orangish yellow with a raised purplish brown center, solitary to few, terminal, individual flowerheads 2–4" (5–10 cm) wide, rimmed with 10–20 somewhat oblong, notch-tipped, petal-like rays. PLANT: 1–3' (30–90 cm) tall; leaves alternate, simple, lance-shaped, margin entire to slightly toothed, green. HABITAT: fields and meadows.

Yellow Goat's-beard / *Tragopogon pratensis*

Dandelion / *Taraxacum officinale*

Elecampane / *Inula helenium*

Coltsfoot / *Tussilago farfara*

Black-eyed Susan / *Rudbeckia hirta*

Cat's Ear / *Hypochaeris radicata*

Sneezeweed

•*Helenium autumnale* L.

•Aster family **Asteraceae**

FLOWERING SEASON: late August–September. FLOWERHEADS: yellow with a raised yellow globular center, several to many, terminal; individual flowerheads 1–2" (2.5–5 cm) wide, rimmed with 10–18 drooping, wedge-shaped, 3-lobed, petal-like rays. PLANT: 2–6' (0.6–1.8 m) tall; leaves alternate, simple, lance-shaped, margin toothed, green. HABITAT: swamps and wet meadows. COMMENTS: *Helenium flexosum*, also known as sneezeweed, is a very similar plant with a raised brownish center.

Atlantic Golden Aster, Sickle-leaved Golden Aster

•*Pityopsis falcata* (Pursh) Nutt.

•Aster family **Asteraceae**

FLOWERING SEASON: late July–October. FLOWERHEADS: yellow, several to many, terminal and axillary, individual flowerheads ¼–½" (6–13 mm) wide, rimmed with usually 10–14 minutely notched petal-like rays. PLANT: 4–12" (10–30 cm) tall; leaves alternate, simple, long and narrow, margin entire, green. HABITAT: dry sandy soil in coastal areas.

LEAVES ALTERNATE, COMPOUND OR DEEPLY LOBED OR DIVIDED

Green-headed Coneflower

•*Rudbeckia laciniata* L.

•Aster family **Asteraceae**

FLOWERING SEASON: late July to early September. FLOWERHEADS: yellow with a raised ovoid greenish yellow center, several, terminal; individual flowerheads 2½–4" (6.3–10 cm) wide, rimmed with 6–10 drooping, somewhat oblong, petal-like rays. PLANT: 3–10' (0.9–3 m) tall; leaves alternate, simple, with 3–7 deeply cleft pinnate lobes, margin large-toothed,

green. HABITAT: moist thickets.

Golden Ragwort

•*Senecio aureus* L.

•Aster family **Asteraceae**

FLOWERING SEASON: May–June. FLOWERHEADS: golden yellow, several to many in terminal clusters; individual flowerheads ⅝–¾" (1.6–2 cm) wide, rimmed with 8–12 minutely toothed petal-like rays surrounding a yellow center. PLANT: 1–2½' (30–76 cm) tall; leaves of 2 types: basal leaves heart-shaped, simple, with long stalks; upper leaves alternate, deeply lobed, clasping; margin toothed, green. HABITAT: swamps, wet meadows, and wet woodlands.

LEAVES ALTERNATE OR OPPOSITE, OFTEN BOTH ON THE SAME PLANT

Thin-leaf Sunflower

•*Helianthus decapetalus* L.

•Aster family **Asteraceae**

FLOWERING SEASON: August–September. FLOWERHEADS: yellow, several, terminal; individual flowerheads about 2½" (6.3 cm) wide, with 8–15 somewhat oblong, petal-like rays. PLANT: 1–5' (0.3–1.5 m) tall; leaves opposite or alternate, simple, broadly lance-shaped with a pointed tip, margin toothed, green. HABITAT: moist woodlands. COMMENTS: a very common woodland sunflower.

Jerusalem Artichoke

•*Helianthus tuberosus* L.

•Aster family **Asteraceae**

FLOWERING SEASON: September to mid-October. FLOWERHEADS: yellow, several, terminal; individual flowerheads about 3" (7.5 cm) wide, rimmed with 12–20 oblong, petal-like rays. PLANT: 6–12' (1.8–3.6 m) tall; leaves opposite and alternate on a rough stem, simple, ovate tapering to a pointed tip, margin toothed, green. HABITAT: creek and

Jerusalem Artichoke / *Helianthus tuberosus*

Golden Ragwort / *Senecio aureus*

Atlantic Golden Aster, Sickle-leaved Golden Aster / *Pityopsis falcata*

Green-headed Coneflower / *Rudbeckia laciniata*

Thin-leaf Sunflower / *Helianthus decapetalus*

Sneezeweed / *Helenium autumnale*

riverbanks and open, moist soil. COM-MENTS: prized for its edible, somewhat potato-like, tuber.

LEAVES OPPOSITE, SIMPLE

Bur-marigold, Stick-tights
•*Bidens cernua* L.
•Aster family **Asteraceae**
FLOWERING SEASON: September. FLOW-ERHEADS: yellow, several to many, termi-nal and upper axial; individual flower-heads ½–1" (1.3–2.5 cm) wide, rimmed with 6–10 short, petal-like rays. PLANT: 1–3' (30–90 cm) tall; leaves opposite, simple, narrowly lance-shaped, margin toothed, green. HABITAT: wet soil.

Lance-leaved Coreopsis
•*Coreopsis lanceolata* L.
•Aster family **Asteraceae**
FLOWERING SEASON: June–August. FLOW-ERHEADS: yellow, solitary to few, termi-nal, individual flowerheads 1½–2½" (3.8–6.3 cm) wide, rimmed with 6–10 toothed, petal-like rays. PLANT: 1–2' (30–60 cm) tall; leaves mostly opposite, simple, narrowly oblong, margin entire, green. HABITAT: meadows.

~

FLOWERS NOT RADIALLY SYMMETRICAL; MINUTE, FILAMENTOUS, TUBULAR WITH NO PETAL-LIKE LOBES, OR WITH NO OBVIOUS PETAL-LIKE PARTS

LACKING TYPICAL LEAVES

Beechdrops
•*Epifagus virginiana* (L.) Bartr.
•Broom-rape family **Orobanchaceae**
FLOWERING SEASON: late August to early October. FLOWERS: yellowish with pur-plish brown stripes, many, alternate along branching stems; about ⁵⁄₁₆" (8 mm) long, tubular with 4 tiny triangu-lar lobes. PLANT: 6–24" (15–60 cm) tall; leaves absent; stem yellowish brown. HABITAT: beech woodlands. COMMENTS: parasitic on beech tree roots.

AQUATIC

Horned Bladderwort
•*Utricularia cornuta* Michx.
•Bladderwort family **Lentibulariaceae**
FLOWERING SEASON: August. FLOWERS: yellow, 1–6, usually paired, terminal; about ¾" (1.9 cm) long, tubular, 2-lipped; upper lip small and erect; lower lip helmet-shaped with a conspicuous spur at the base. PLANT: aquatic, 3–10" (7.5–25 cm) tall; leaves submerged along an underwater stem, filamentous with small globular bladders. HABITAT: edges of ponds, fens, and other bodies of water. COMMENTS: the leaf bladders function to trap minute aquatic animals for food. Several other yellow bladder-wort species also occur in this region.

Swollen Bladderwort
•*Utricularia inflata* Walt.
•Bladderwort family **Lentibulariaceae**
FLOWERING SEASON: July–early October. FLOWERS: yellow, 1–10, terminal, about ¾" (1.9 cm) wide, tubular and 2-lipped; upper lip broadly ovate; lower lip 3-lobed. PLANT: aquatic, 3–20" (7.5–50 cm) tall; leaves submerged along an underwater stem, filamentous; upper leaves arranged palmately around the stem, with small globular bladders that float the leaves near the surface. HABITAT: ponds.

Bur-marigold, Stick-tights / *Bidens cernua*

Beechdrops / *Epifagus virginiana*

Lance-leaved Coreopsis / *Coreopsis lanceolata*

Horned Bladderwort / *Utricularia cornuta*

Swollen Bladderwort / *Utricularia inflata*

LEAVES BASAL, SIMPLE

Golden-club
•*Orontium aquaticum* L.
•Arum family **Araceae**
FLOWERING SEASON: late April–May.
FLOWERS: minute, many, clustered on a
cylindrical 6–24" (15–60 cm) spike, the
upper flowering portion bright yellow,
the lower portion white. PLANT: 6–24"
(15–60 cm) tall; leaves basal, simple,
lance-shaped and long-stalked, margin
entire, green. HABITAT: swamps, ponds,
and fens, often in standing water.

LEAVES ALTERNATE, SIMPLE

Yellow Violet
•*Viola pubescens* Ait.
•Violet family **Violaceae**
FLOWERING SEASON: May. FLOWERS: yellow with purple veining, few, terminal;
up to ¾" (1.9 cm) wide, with 5 unequal
rounded petals. PLANT: 5–20" (12.5–
50 cm) tall; leaves basal and alternate,
simple, broadly heart-shaped, margin
toothed, green. HABITAT: woodlands.

Spotted Jewelweed, Touch-me-not
•*Impatiens capensis* Meerb.
•Touch-me-not family **Balsaminaceae**
FLOWERING SEASON: mid-July to early
September. FLOWERS: orange-yellow
mottled with reddish brown, solitary to
several in leaf axils; ¾–1" (1.9–2.5 cm)
long, tubular with a prominent curved
basal spur and showy frontal lobes.
PLANT: 2–5' (0.6–1.5 m) tall; leaves alternate, simple, ovate to elliptic, margin
toothed, green. HABITAT: moist soil.

Pale Jewelweed, Touch-me-not
•*Impatiens pallida* Nutt.
•Touch-me-not family **Balsaminaceae**
FLOWERING SEASON: July–August. FLOW-
ERS: pale yellow to yellow, sparingly mottled with reddish brown dots or dotless,
solitary to several in leaf axils; 1–1¼"
(2.5–3.1 cm) long, tubular with a prominent curved basal spur and showy frontal
lobes. PLANT: 2–5' (0.6–1.5 m) tall;
leaves alternate, simple, ovate to elliptic,
margin toothed, green. HABITAT: moist
soil.

Butter-and-eggs
•*Linaria vulgaris* Mill.
•Figwort family **Scrophulariaceae**
FLOWERING SEASON: mid-June through
August. FLOWERS: pale yellow with
orange on a portion of the lower lip,
several in a narrow densely flowered
terminal cluster; about 1–1¼" (2.5–
3.1 cm) long, tubular with 2 lips and a
long basal spur. PLANT: 1–2' (30–60 cm)
tall; leaves alternate, simple, long and
narrow, margin entire, green. HABITAT:
fields, roadsides, and waste areas.

Wood-betony, Lousewort
•*Pedicularis canadensis* L.
•Figwort family **Scrophulariaceae**
FLOWERING SEASON: mid-May to early
June. FLOWERS: bicolored, yellow and
purplish brown, several in a dense terminal cluster; about ¾" (1.9 cm) long,
tubular, 2-lipped; upper lip large and
hood-shaped; lower lip 3-lobed. PLANT:
6–18" (15–45 cm) tall; leaves mostly
alternate, simple, oblong and many-
lobed, margin bluntly toothed, green.
HABITAT: woodlands and along streams.

Butter-and-eggs / *Linaria vulgaris*

Wood-betony, Lousewort / *Pedicularis canadensis*

Pale Jewelweed, Touch-me-not / *Impatiens pallida*

Spotted Jewelweed, Touch-me-not / *Impatiens capensis*

Golden-club / *Orontium aquaticum*

Yellow Violet / *Viola pubescens*

Blue-stem Goldenrod
• *Solidago caesia* L.
• Aster family **Asteraceae**

FLOWERING SEASON: September into October. FLOWERHEADS: yellow, many, in short axial clusters; individual flowerheads up to ¼" (6 mm) high, rimmed with 5 tiny petal-like rays. PLANT: 1–3' (30–90 cm) tall; leaves alternate on a bluish to purple stem, simple, lance-shaped, margin sharply toothed, green. HABITAT: woodlands and thickets.

Late Goldenrod
• *Solidago gigantea* Ait.
• Aster family **Asteraceae**

FLOWERING SEASON: August–September. FLOWERHEADS: yellow, many in a showy branching terminal cluster; individual flowerheads about ¼" (6 mm) high, rimmed with 7–15 tiny, petal-like rays. PLANT: 3–8' (0.9–2.4 m) tall; leaves alternate on a smooth stem, simple, lance-shaped, margin sharply toothed, green. HABITAT: open moist soil. COMMENTS: Canada goldenrod, *Solidago canadensis*, a very similar species of drier soils, has a pubescent stem and flowerheads about ⅛" (3 mm) high.

Yellow Lady's Slipper
• *Cypripedium parviflorum* Salisb.
• Orchid family **Orchidaceae**

FLOWERING SEASON: mid-May to mid-June. FLOWERS: lip yellow, sepals and petals from yellowish green (var. pubescens) to dark reddish brown (var. parviflorum and makasin), 1–2, terminal; lip about ¾–1¼" (1.9–3.1 cm) long in var. parviflorum and makasin, up to about 2" (5 cm) long in var. pubescens, pouch-like. PLANT: 1–2' (30–60 cm) tall; leaves 3–5, alternate, simple, lance-shaped to nearly round, margin entire, green. HABITAT: variable, from dry to more often moist woodlands, swamps, and wooded fens.

Yellow Fringed Orchid
• *Platanthera ciliaris* (L.) Lindl.
• Orchid family **Orchidaceae**

FLOWERING SEASON: July–September. FLOWERS: yellowish orange, 25–50 in a slender terminal cluster; about ⅘" (20 mm) tall, with 5 small petal-like parts and a large, single-lobed, heavily fringed lip with a slender basal spur. PLANT: 1–2½' (30–76 cm) tall; leaves alternate, single, lance-shaped, margin entire, green. HABITAT: variable, from moist meadows to woodlands and roadsides.

Redroot
• *Lachnanthes caroliana* (Lam.) Dandy
• Redroot family **Haemodoraceae**

FLOWERING SEASON: July–August. FLOWERS: cream-yellow, many in a densely flowered terminal cluster, individual flowers about ⅓" (8.3 mm) wide, filamentous, without obvious petal-like parts. PLANT: 1½–2½' (45–76 cm) tall; leaves basal and alternate, simple, long and narrow, margin entire, green. HABITAT: swamps, pond edges, and open moist soils. COMMENTS: rare. The common name refers to the bright-colored sap.

LEAVES ALTERNATE, COMPOUND OR DEEPLY DIVIDED

Early Meadow-rue
• *Thalictrum dioicum* L.
• Crowfoot family **Ranunculaceae**

FLOWERING SEASON: late April to mid-May. FLOWERS: greenish to yellowish, several to many in a terminal cluster; about ¼" (6 mm) long, composed of a tassel-like mass of yellowish thread-like stamens and about 5 tiny petal-like sepals. PLANT: 1–2' (30–60 cm) tall; leaves alternate, compound with numerous leaflets; leaflets rounded with 5–9 lobes, green. HABITAT: woodlands.

Yellow Fringed Orchid / *Platanthera ciliaris*

Late Goldenrod / *Solidago gigantea*

Yellow Lady's Slipper / *Cypripedium parviflorum*

Redroot / *Lachnanthes caroliana*

Early Meadow-rue / *Thalictrum dioicum*

Blue-stem Goldenrod / *Solidago caesia*

Low Hop Clover

- *Trifolium campestre* Schreb.
- Bean family **Fabaceae**

FLOWERING SEASON: June–September. **FLOWERHEADS:** yellow, several, axillary, globular to oval, ⅓–½" (8.3–13 mm) long, composed of 15–40 tiny yellow individual flowers. **PLANT:** often somewhat prostrate; leaves alternate, compound with 3 leaflets; leaflets obovate, margins minutely toothed, green. **HABITAT:** meadows and roadsides.

Wild Indigo

- *Baptisia tinctoria* (L.) Vent.
- Bean family **Fabaceae**

FLOWERING SEASON: July–early August. **FLOWERS:** yellow, many, in few to several flowered terminal clusters; about ½" (1.3 cm) long, pea-like. **PLANT:** 2–4' (0.6–1.2 m) tall; leaves alternate, compound with 3 leaflets; leaflets obovate, margins entire, green. **HABITAT:** roadsides, open woodlands, and meadows.

Scotch Broom

- *Cytisus scoparius* (L.) Lam.
- Bean family **Fabaceae**

FLOWERING SEASON: late May–June. **FLOWERS:** yellow, several to many, in elongated terminal clusters; about 1" (2.5 cm) long, pea-like. **PLANT:** 3–5' (0.9–1.5 m) tall; leaves alternate, mostly compound with 3 leaflets; leaflets obovate, small, margins entire, green. **HABITAT:** sandy soils and waste areas.

Partridge Pea

- *Chamaecrista fasciculata* (Michx.) Greene
- Bean family **Fabaceae**

FLOWERING SEASON: late July to early September. **FLOWERS:** yellow, often purple-spotted near the base, several, 2–4 in axillary groups; about 1–1½" (2.5–3.8 cm) wide, with 5 unequal rounded petals. **PLANT:** 1–2½' (30–76 cm) tall; leaves alternate, pinnately compound with 20–30 leaflets; leaflets oblong, margins entire, green. **HABITAT:** meadows, most frequently coastal.

Bird's-foot Trefoil

- *Lotus corniculata* L.
- Bean family **Fabaceae**

FLOWERING SEASON: late May into September. **FLOWERS:** yellow, many, 3–12 in rounded clusters scattered throughout the plant; about ⅝" (1.6 cm) long, pea-like. **PLANT:** trailing or ascending, 3–24" (7.5–60 cm) long; leaves alternate, compound with 3 leaflets; leaflets obovate, margins entire, green. **HABITAT:** meadows, roadsides, and waste areas. **COMMENTS:** seeds in several slender pods that resemble a bird's foot.

Yellow Sweet-clover

- *Melilotus altissima* Thuill.
- Bean family **Fabaceae**

FLOWERING SEASON: June–August. **FLOWERS:** yellow, many, in slender 2–4" (5–10 cm) long, often 1-sided axial clusters; about ¼" (6 mm) long, narrowly pea-like. **PLANT:** 3–5' (0.9–1.5 m) tall; leaves alternate, compound with 3 leaflets; leaflets narrowly oblong, margin toothed, green. **HABITAT:** fields, roadsides, and waste areas.

Wild Indigo / *Baptisia tinctoria*

Bird's-foot Trefoil / *Lotus corniculata*

Scotch Broom / *Cytisus scoparius*

Yellow Sweet-clover / *Melilotus altissima*

Low Hop Clover / *Trifolium campestre*

Partridge Pea / *Chamaecrista fasciculata*

Yellow Thistle
•*Cirsium horridulum* Michx.
•Aster family **Asteraceae**
FLOWERING SEASON: June–July. FLOWER-HEADS: pale yellow or purplish, several, terminal and upper axillary, individual flowerheads 2–4" (5–10 cm) wide, filamentous, base of flowerhead urn-shaped and clasped by spiny upper leaves. PLANT: 2–5' (0.6–1.5 m) tall; leaves alternate, simple, deeply pinnately lobed, margin with stiff spines, green. HABITAT: moist to dry fields and roadsides.

Pineapple-weed
•*Matricaria discoidea* DC.
•Aster family **Asteraceae**
FLOWERING SEASON: late May into August. FLOWERHEADS: greenish yellow, many, terminal and axial; individual flowerheads up to 5/16" (8 mm) wide, appearing like a small daisy without petals. PLANT: 6–18" (15–45 cm) tall; leaves alternate, simple, pinnately divided into many narrow lobes, margin toothed, green; giving off a pineapple-like fragrance when torn. HABITAT: waste areas, meadows, and roadsides.

LEAVES OPPOSITE, SIMPLE

Horse-balm
•*Collinsonia canadensis* L.
•Mint family **Lamiaceae**
FLOWERING SEASON: August. FLOWERS: light yellow, several to many in a loose terminal cluster; about ½" (1.3 cm) long, tubular with 2 lips; upper lip 3-lobed; lower lip 2-lobed; lemony fragrance. PLANT: 2–5' (0.6–1.5 m) tall; leaves opposite on a square stem, simple, ovate, margin coarsely and sharply toothed, green. HABITAT: moist woodlands.

Dotted Horsemint
•*Monarda punctata* L.
•Mint family **Lamiaceae**
FLOWERING SEASON: late July to early September. FLOWERS: yellowish with purple spots, many, in circular axillary or terminal clusters; about 1" (2.5 cm) long, tubular with 2 elongated lips; upper lip 2-lobed; lower lip 3-lobed. PLANT: 2–3' (60–90 cm) tall; leaves opposite on a square stem, simple, lance-shaped, margin toothed, green. HABITAT: sandy soils, frequently found near the ocean.

Rattlebox, Yellow Rattle
•*Rhinanthus crista-galli* L.
•Figwort family **Scrophulariaceae**
FLOWERING SEASON: late June to July. FLOWERS: yellow, several in a terminal, usually 1-sided cluster; ½–¾" (1.3–2 cm) long, tubular, 2-lipped; upper lip large and hood-shaped; lower lip 3-lobed. PLANT: 6–18" (15–46 cm) tall; leaves opposite, simple, broadly lance-shaped, margin coarsely toothed, green. HABITAT: meadows. COMMENTS: the base of the flower swells into a bladder-like capsule in which the seeds rattle when ripe.

Golden Pert, Golden Hedge-hyssop
•*Gratiola aurea* Muhl.
•Figwort family **Scrophulariaceae**
FLOWERING SEASON: mid-June to mid-September. FLOWERS: bright yellow, several, axillary; about ½" (1.3 cm) long, tubular with 4 petal-like lobes. PLANT: stems may be partially prostrate and partially erect, 3–8" (7.5–20 cm) long; leaves opposite, simple, ovate to obovate, margin slightly toothed, green. HABITAT: along ponds and lakes and in open moist areas. COMMENTS: often associated with vernal ponds.

Horse-balm / *Collinsonia canadensis*

Pineapple-weed / *Matricaria discoidea*

Rattlebox, Yellow Rattle / *Rhinanthus crista-galli*

Golden Pert, Golden Hedge-hyssop / *Gratiola aurea*

Dotted Horsemint / *Monarda punctata*

Yellow Thistle / *Cirsium horridulum*

Bush Honeysuckle
•*Diervilla lonicera* Mill.
•Honeysuckle family **Caprifoliaceae**
FLOWERING SEASON: June. **FLOWERS:** yellow, 1–5 in terminal clusters; about ¾"
(1.9 cm) long, tubular with 5 recurved petal-like lobes. **PLANT:** shrub, 2–4'
(0.6–1.2 m) tall; leaves opposite, simple, lance-shaped, margin minutely toothed, green. **HABITAT:** woodlands.

Early Fly Honeysuckle
•*Lonicera canadensis* Bartr.
•Honeysuckle family **Caprifoliaceae**
FLOWERING SEASON: May. **FLOWERS:** yellow to greenish yellow, in axial pairs; about ¾" (2 cm) long, funnel-shaped with 5 equal lobes. **PLANT:** shrub, 2–5'
(0.6–1.5 m) tall; leaves opposite, simple, oval, margin entire, green. **HABITAT:**
woodlands.

Tartarian Honeysuckle
•*Lonicera tartarica* L.
•Honeysuckle family **Caprifoliaceae**
FLOWERING SEASON: mid-May to mid-June. **FLOWERS:** pink to white or yellowish, many, in axial pairs; about ¾"
(1.9 cm) long, tubular with 5 unequal, narrow, petal-like lobes. **PLANT:** shrub,
5–10' (1.5–3 m) tall; leaves opposite, simple, ovate, margin entire, green.
HABITAT: hedgerows, thickets, and open woodlots.

Japanese Honeysuckle
•*Lonicera japonica* Thunb.
•Honeysuckle family **Caprifoliaceae**
FLOWERING SEASON: July–August. **FLOWERS:** white to yellow, in pairs in upper axils; about 1" (2.5 cm) long, tubular, 2-lipped, upper lip narrow, 1-lobed, recurved; lower lip broad, 4-lobed, recurved. **PLANT:** vine-like; leaves opposite, simple, ovate, margin entire, green.

HABITAT: woodlands, swamps, and thickets. **COMMENTS:** escaped from cultivation and sometimes a serious pest.

Bush Honeysuckle / *Diervilla lonicera*

Early Fly Honeysuckle / *Lonicera canadensis*

Tartarian Honeysuckle / *Lonicera tartarica*

Japanese Honeysuckle / *Lonicera japonica*

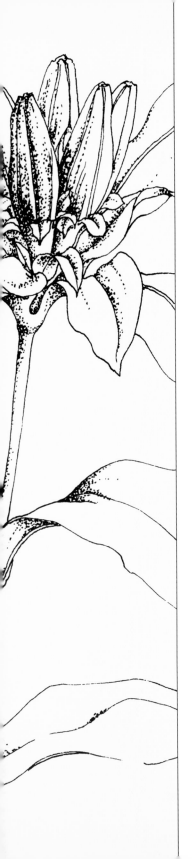

PART FOUR

GREEN FLOWERS

FLOWERS SYMMETRICAL, WITH 5 PETALS OR PETAL-LIKE PARTS

LEAVES BASAL, SIMPLE

Naked Miterwort
• *Mitella nuda* L.
• Saxifrage family **Saxifragaceae**
FLOWERING SEASON: May–June. **FLOW-ERS:** cream to pale green, several on an erect wand-like cluster; about ⅙" (4.2 mm) wide, with 5 feathery petals. **PLANT:** 3–7" (7.5–17.5 cm) tall; leaves mostly basal, simple, rounded with a heart-shaped base, margin scalloped, green. **HABITAT:** moist woods and swamps.

LEAVES ALTERNATE, SIMPLE

Oriental Bittersweet
• *Celastrus orbiculata* Thunb.
• Staff-tree family **Celastraceae**
FLOWERING SEASON: June. **FLOWERS:** green, many, in terminal and axillary clusters; about ⅛" (4 mm) wide, with 5 petal-like parts. **PLANT:** woody vine, 25' (7.5 m) or more long; leaves alternate, simple, nearly round, margin toothed, green; fruit scarlet, enclosed in open orange capsule coverings. **HABITAT:** woodlands, hedgerows, and roadsides. **COMMENTS:** a seriously invasive nuisance. The practice of making holiday wreaths from this vine is being discouraged out of concern for misidentification with the declining American bittersweet, *Celastrus scandens*, which has similar fruit but narrower leaves and terminal flower clusters.

LEAVES ALTERNATE, COMPOUND OR DEEPLY DEVIDED

Poison Ivy
• *Toxicodendron radicans* (L.) Kuntze
• Sumac family **Anacardiaceae**
FLOWERING SEASON: June. **FLOWERS:** green, many in 1–3" (2.5–7.5 cm) long, loose axial clusters; about ⅛" (3 mm) wide, with 5 tiny rounded petals. **PLANT:** woody vine, up to 20' (6 m) or more long; leaves alternate, compound with 3 leaflets; leaflets ovate, margins entire or with a few large teeth, green. **HABITAT:** swamps, woodlands, and roadsides. **COMMENTS:** *contact with any part of this plant may cause severe dermatitis.*

Poison Sumac
• *Toxicodendron vernix* (L.) Kuntze
• Sumac family **Anacardiaceae**
FLOWERING SEASON: June. **FLOWERS:** pale green to white, many, in loosely flowered 3–8" (7.5–20 cm) long clusters; minute, with 5 petals. **PLANT:** shrub or small tree; leaves alternate, pinnately compound with 7–13 leaflets; leaflets obovate to oval, margins entire, green; fruit white, globular, smooth, in a loose, drooping cluster. **HABITAT:** swamps, often growing in shallow water. **COMMENTS:** *caution, poisonous to touch.* Staghorn sumac, *Rhus hirta*, has ⅒" (2.5 mm) wide yellowish green, 5-petaled flowers in dense, erect clusters, toothed leaflets, and hairy reddish fruit in upright clusters.

Staghorn Sumac / *Rhus hirta*

Poison Sumac / *Toxicodendron vernix*

Poison Ivy / *Toxicodendron radicans*

Naked Miterwort / *Mitella nuda*

Oriental Bittersweet / *Celastrus orbiculata*

Angelica
•*Angelica atropurpurea* L.
•Carrot family **Apiaceae**
FLOWERING SEASON: mid-June to early July. FLOWER: pale green to greenish white, many in spherical terminal clusters up to 10" (25 cm) wide; individual flowers minute, with 5 tiny petals. PLANT: 4–6' (1.2–1.8 m) tall; leaves alternate, with several pinnately compound divisions; leaflets ovate with pointed tips, margins toothed, green; stem purple. HABITAT: swamps and moist meadows.

LEAVES OPPOSITE, SIMPLE

Poke Milkweed
•*Asclepias exaltata* L.
•Milkweed family **Asclepiadaceae**
FLOWERING SEASON: June–July. FLOWERS: white and green, several to many, in loosely flowered rounded terminal and upper axillary clusters; about ¼–⅓" (6–8.3 mm) long, with 5 deeply recurved green petals and a 5-pointed white crown-like center. PLANT: 3–6' (0.9–1.8 m) tall; leaves opposite, simple, oval to ovate, margin entire, green. HABITAT: thickets and woodlands.

LEAVES WHORLED, COMPOUND

Ginseng
•*Panax quinquefolius* L.
•Ginseng family **Araliaceae**
FLOWERING SEASON: late June to mid-July. FLOWERS: yellowish green, 6–20 in a small, rounded terminal cluster; about ¹⁄₁₆" (1.6 mm) wide, with 5 inconspicuous petals and 5 prominent stamens. PLANT: 8–15" (20–37.5 cm) tall; leaves 3, whorled about the stem, palmately compound with 5 leaflets; leaflets ovate with a pointed tip, margins irregularly toothed, green. HABITAT: woodlands. COMMENTS: *commercially exploited; do not disturb.*

FLOWERS SYMMETRICAL, WITH 6 PETALS OR PETAL-LIKE PARTS

LEAVES ALTERNATE, SIMPLE

Carrion-flower
•*Smilax herbacea* L.
•Greenbrier family **Smilacaceae**
FLOWERING SEASON: June. FLOWERS: green, many in rounded, long-stemmed axial clusters; about ⅜" (9 cm) wide, with 6 narrowly lance-shaped petal-like divisions and several conspicuous, filamentous, white-tipped stamens; unpleasantly fragrant. PLANT: climbing vine, 3–6' (0.9–1.8 m) long; leaves alternate on a smooth herbaceous stem, simple, ovate, often with a slightly heart-shaped base, margin entire, green. HABITAT: woodlands, thickets, and along waterways. COMMENTS: the common name refers to the flowers' odor of rotten meat. Other *Smilax* species have armed woody stems: the stem of the bristly greenbrier, *S. hispida*, is covered with numerous tiny prickles; the stem of horse-brier, *S. rotundifolia*, has fewer thorns, which are stout, flattened, and rose-like.

False Hellebore
•*Veratrum viride* Ait.
•Lily family **Liliaceae**
FLOWERING SEASON: mid-June to mid-July. FLOWERS: yellowish green, many in an 8–24" (20–60 cm) branching terminal cluster; up to 1" (2.5 cm) wide, perianth with 6 oblong, petal-like parts. PLANT: 2–8' (0.6–2.4 m) tall; leaves alternate, simple, broadly oval, margin entire, green. HABITAT: swamps and wet woods.

False Hellebore / *Veratrum viride*

Carrion-flower / *Smilax herbacea*

Poke Milkweed / *Asclepias exaltata*

Angelica / *Angelica atropurpurea*

Ginseng / *Panax quinquefolius*

FLOWERS NOT RADIALLY SYMMETRICAL; MINUTE, FILAMENTOUS, TUBULAR WITH NO PETAL-LIKE LOBES, OR WITH NO OBVIOUS PETAL-LIKE PARTS

LEAVES BASAL, SIMPLE

Narrow-leaf Cattail
•*Typha angustifolia* L.
•Cattail family **Typhaceae**
FLOWERING SEASON: June. FLOWERS: yellowish green, many on a 6–24" (15–61 cm) tall 2-sectioned slender, cylindrical terminal spike; staminate flowers on the upper section; pistillate flowers on the lower sections; individual flowers tiny. PLANT: 4–8' (1.2–2.4 m) tall; leaves basal, simple, very long and narrow, margin entire, green. HABITAT: marshes, edges of ponds, lakes, creeks, rivers, and moist soil.

Loesel's Twayblade
•*Liparis loeselii* (L.) L. Rich.
•Orchid family **Orchidaceae**
FLOWERING SEASON: late June to mid-July. FLOWERS: yellowish green, 2–12 in a loose, slender terminal cluster; about ⅜" (10 mm) tall, with 5 very narrow petals and sepals and an oblong lip. PLANT: 2–8" (5–20 cm) tall; leaves 2, basal, simple, oblong, margin entire, green. HABITAT: moist soils (from fens to roadside ditches).

White Malaxis, White Adder's Mouth
•*Malaxis brachypoda* (Gray) Fernald
•Orchid family **Orchidaceae**
FLOWERING SEASON: June early August. FLOWERS: greenish white to yellowish green, 6–50, on a slender terminal cluster; about ⅛" (1.6 mm) tall, with 6 unequal petal-like parts. PLANT: 3–6" (7.5–15 cm) tall; leaf solitary, basal, simple, obovate, margin entire, green. HABITAT: moist woodlands. COMMENTS: the region's smallest wild orchid flower.

Sweetflag, Calamus
•*Acorus americanus* (Raf.) Raf.
•Arum family **Araceae**
FLOWERING SEASON: late May–June. FLOWERS: yellowish green, minute, many clustered on a 2–3½" (5–8.8 cm) long, finger-like projection found on the lower third of a leaf-like flower stem. PLANT: 2–6' (0.6–1.8 m) tall; leaves basal, simple, long and narrow, margin entire, pale green. HABITAT: swamps, moist meadows, and along streams.

Arrowleaf, Tuckahoe, Arrow Arum
•*Peltandra virginica* (L.) Schott ex Schott and Endl.
•Arum family **Araceae**
FLOWERING SEASON: mid-June to mid-July. FLOWERS: minute, many on an erect cylindrical spike almost entirely enclosed in a green 4–8" (10–20 cm) tall sheath that appears like a rolled-up leaf. PLANT: 6–30" (15–75 cm) tall; leaves basal, simple, arrowhead-shaped and long-stemmed, margin entire, green. HABITAT: swamps, drainage ditches, edges of ponds and lakes, often in standing water.

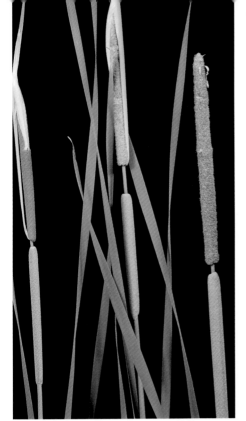

Narrow-leaf Cattail / *Typha angustifolia*

Sweetflag, Calamus / *Acorus americanus*

Loesel's Twayblade / *Liparis loeselii*

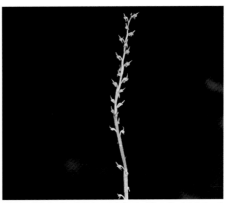

White Malaxis, White Adder's Mouth / *Malaxis brachypoda*

Arrowleaf, Tuckahoe, Arrow Arum / *Peltandra virginica*

LEAVES BASAL, COMPOUND OR DEEPLY DIVIDED

Jack-in-the-pulpit
•*Arisaema triphyllum* (L.) Schott ex Schott and Endl.
•Arum family **Araceae**
FLOWERING SEASON: May–early June. FLOWERS: minute, many clustered on an erect, finger-like projection enclosed by a leaf-like sheath; sheath appearing tubular at the base, the upper portion arching forward over the flowering spike, green, usually with purple stripes. PLANT: 10–36" (25–90 cm) tall; leaves 1 or 2, basal, long-stalked, each with 3 leaflets; leaflets broadly lance-shaped, margins entire, green. HABITAT: woodlands.

Green Dragon, Dragon-root
•*Arisaema dracontium* (L.) Schott ex Schott and Endl.
•Arum family **Araceae**
FLOWERING SEASON: June. FLOWERS: minute, many on an erect 1–2" (2.5–5 cm) long, cylindrical yellowish spike tapering upward another 7" (18 cm) above the flowering portion, the lower portion enclosed in a leaf-like sheath. PLANT: 8–32" (20–80 cm) tall; leaf usually solitary, basal, long-stalked, with 5–17 leaflets in the upper portion, which is usually oriented parallel to the ground; leaflets mostly arranged on the same side of the stalk, oblong, margins entire, green. HABITAT: moist woodlands and along streams.

LEAVES ALTERNATE, SIMPLE

Creeping Snowberry
•*Gaultheria hispidula* (L.) Muhl. ex Bigel.
•Heath family **Ericaceae**
FLOWERING SEASON: May. FLOWERS: green, few, individually axillary, minute, without obvious petal-like parts, nodding. PLANT: prostrate shrub, branches 3–12" (7.5–30 cm) long; leaves alternate, simple, oval to ovate, margin entire, green, odor of wintergreen when crushed; fruit a smooth-skinned edible white berry, about ⅓" (8.3) mm) wide. HABITAT: moist woodlands, bogs, and fens.

Frost Grape
•*Vitis riparia* Michx.
•Grape family **Vitaceae**
FLOWERING SEASON: June. FLOWERS: pale green, many in loose axial clusters about 3" (7.5 cm) long; individual flowers minute. PLANT: woody vine, up to 25' (7.5 m) or more long; leaves alternate, simple, broadly ovate with 3–7 lobes, margin coarsely toothed, green, smooth on both surfaces. HABITAT: hedgerows, woodlands, and riverbanks. COMMENTS: fox grape, *Vitis lambrusca*, which has many cultivated varieties, has broader leaves with a densely pubescent lower surface. The fruit of both wild and domestic grapes is edible.

Clotbur, Common Cocklebur
•*Xanthium strumarium* L.
•Aster family **Asteraceae**
FLOWERING SEASON: mid-August through September. FLOWERHEADS: green, minute, enclosed in oblong ½–¾" (1.3–2 cm) long burrs; burrs covered with many slender hooked prickles and tipped with 2 beak-like structures. PLANT: 1–6' (0.3–1.8 m) tall; leaves alternate, simple, broad and maple-like, margin toothed, green. HABITAT: waste areas.

Green Dragon, Dragon-root / *Arisaema dracontium*

Clotbur, Common Cocklebur / *Xanthium strumarium*

Creeping Snowberry / *Gaultheria hispidula*

Frost Grape / *Vitis riparia*

Jack-in-the-pulpit / *Arisaema triphyllum*

Small Solomon's Seal
•*Polygonatum biflorum* (Walt.) Ell.
•Lily family **Liliaceae**
FLOWERING SEASON: late May to early June. **FLOWERS:** yellowish green, several, found singly or in pairs (occasionally in groups of 3 or 4) in axils; about ½" (1.3 cm) long, tubularly bell-shaped with 6 small pointed teeth, pendant. **PLANT:** 8–36" (20–90 cm) long; leaves alternate, simple, broadly lance-shaped, margin entire, green. **HABITAT:** woodlands. **COMMENTS:** hairy Solomon's seal, *Polygonatum pubescens*, has hairy veins on the underside of the leaves. *Polygonatum biflorum* has smooth veins.

Helleborine Orchid
•*Epipactis helleborine* (L.) Crantz
•Orchid family **Orchidaceae**
FLOWERING SEASON: mid-July to late August. **FLOWERS:** pale to olive-green with reddish brown tints, 15–35 or more in a slender terminal cluster; about ⅗" (15 cm) tall and wide, with 5 broadly lance-shaped, petal-like parts and a cup-shaped lip. **PLANT:** 10–24" (25–60 cm) or more tall; leaves alternate, simple, broadly lance-shaped, margin entire, green. **HABITAT:** woodlands.

Bayard's Malaxis
•*Malaxis bayardii* Fern.
•Orchid family **Orchidaceae**
FLOWERING SEASON: July and August. **FLOWERS:** green to yellowish green, with up to 50 flowers in a tall, cylindrical terminal cluster; about ¼" (6 mm) tall; with 6 petal-like parts, including a prominent, deeply notched lip with somewhat horn-like lobes at the base. **PLANT:** 4–10" (10–25 cm) tall; leaf solitary on the stem, simple, broadly obovate, margin entire, green. **HABITAT:** sandy or rocky soil in dry woodlands. **COMMENTS:** green adder's-mouth, *Malaxis unifolia*, which has a funnel-shaped flower cluster and a lip that is heart-shaped at the base, is found in moister soils.

LEAVES ALTERNATE, COMPOUND OR DEEPLY DIVIDED

European Burnet
•*Sanguisorba minor* Scop.
•Rose family **Rosaceae**
FLOWERING SEASON: June–July. **FLOWERS:** light green, many, in ½" (1.3 cm) wide rounded terminal clusters, individual flowers with prominent filamentous stamens over 4 inconspicuous petal-like parts. **PLANT:** 10–20" (25–50 cm) tall; leaves alternate, pinnately compound with 7–19 leaflets; leaflets ovate to broadly oval, margins toothed, green. **HABITAT:** meadows and roadsides.

Common Mugwort, Wormwood
•*Artemisia vulgaris* L.
•Aster family **Asteraceae**
FLOWERING SEASON: late August–September. **FLOWERHEADS:** greenish, many in the upper leaf axils; individual flowerheads about ³⁄₁₆" (4 mm) wide, oblong. **PLANT:** 1–3½' (0.3–1.1 m) tall; leaves alternate, pinnately compound into sharply toothed lobes, margins coarsely toothed, dark green above, white and densely tomentose beneath. **HABITAT:** waste areas.

Common Mugwort, Wormwood / *Artemisia vulgaris*

Helleborine Orchid / *Epipactis helleborine*

European Burnet / *Sanguisorba minor*

Bayard's Malaxis / *Malaxis bayardii*

Small Solomon's Seal / *Polygonatum biflorum*

Dusty-miller, Beach Wormwood
- *Artemisia stelleriana* Besser
- Aster family Asteraceae

FLOWERING SEASON: June–September. FLOWERHEADS: yellowish green, many, in numerous slender terminal and axillary clusters, individual flowerheads about 1/10" (2.5 mm) wide, hemispheric, without obvious petal-like parts, nodding. PLANT: 2–5' (0.6–1.5 m) tall; leaves alternate, simple with deeply pinnately arranged lobes, green covered with a pale pubescence. HABITAT: sandy soils, usually coastal.

LEAVES ALTERNATE AND OPPOSITE ON THE SAME PLANT, DEEPLY DIVIDED

Marijuana, Hemp
- *Cannabis sativa* L.
- Hemp family Cannabaceae

FLOWERING SEASON: July–August. FLOWERS: green, many, axillary; dioecious (male and female flowers different); male flowers tiny, in narrow, drooping clusters; female flowers tiny, erect, filamentous, about 1" (2.5 cm) tall. PLANT: 3–10' (0.9–3 m) tall; leaves alternate and opposite on the same plant, so deeply divided as to appear palmately compound, segments long and narrow, margins toothed, green. HABITAT: fields, woodlands, and waste areas.

Ragweed
- *Ambrosia artemisiifolia* L.
- Aster family Asteraceae

FLOWERING SEASON: mid-August to mid-September. FLOWERHEADS: yellowish green, many, in 1–6" (2.5–15 cm) long, slender terminal, and upper axial clusters; individual flowerheads about 3/16" (5 mm) wide. PLANT: 1–6' (0.3–1.8 m) tall; upper leaves alternate, lower leaves mostly opposite, simple, oblong to lance-shaped, margin deeply pinnately cleft and coarsely toothed, green. HABITAT: fields, roadsides, and waste areas.

LEAVES WHORLED, SIMPLE

Small Whorled Pogonia
- *Isotria medeoloides* (Pursh) Rafinesque
- Orchid family Orchidaceae

FLOWERING SEASON: late May–June. FLOWERS: green, solitary or 2, terminal; about 1¼" (3 cm) tall, center of flower appearing tubular and about ¾" (2 cm) long, framed by 3 narrow petal-like sepals. PLANT: 8–10" (20–25 cm) tall; leaves 5–6 in a single whorl, simple, broadly lance-shaped, margin entire, green. HABITAT: moist woods. COMMENTS: *endangered; do not disturb*. Often overlooked due to the inconspicuous coloration. Report any sightings to the state conservation department.

Large Whorled Pogonia
- *Isotria verticillata* (Muhl. ex Willd.) Raf.
- Orchid family Orchidaceae

FLOWERING SEASON: late May–early June. FLOWER: greenish yellow, solitary, terminal; about 2¾" (6.9 cm) tall, center of flower appearing tubular, about ¾" (1.9 cm) long, framed by 3 very long and narrow brownish sepals. PLANT: 5–12" (12.5–30 cm) tall; leaves 5 or 6 in a single whorl, simple, broadly lance-shaped, margin entire, green. HABITAT: damp to dry woodlands and swampy edges of fens.

Dusty-miller, Beach Wormwood / *Artemisia stelleriana*

Small Whorled Pogonia / *Isotria medeoloides*

Large Whorled Pogonia / *Isotria verticillata*

Ragweed / *Ambrosia artemisiifolia*

Marijuana, Hemp / *Cannabis sativa*

LEAVES WHORLED, COMPOUND

Wild Sarsaparilla
•*Aralia nudicaulis* L.
•Ginseng family **Araliaceae**
FLOWERING SEASON: mid-May to mid-June. FLOWERS: greenish, many, on each of usually 3 circular clusters arising from a single stalk; about ⅛" (3 mm) wide, inconspicuous. PLANT: 12–15" (30–45 cm) tall; leaf solitary, basal, divided so as to appear as 3 whorled, pinnately compound leaves; leaflets usually 5 per section, of unequal size, ovate with a pointed tip, margins toothed, green. HABITAT: woodlands.

Wild Sarsaparilla / *Aralia nudicaulis*

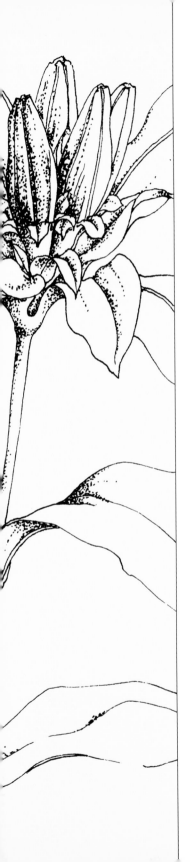

PART FIVE

BLUE TO VIOLET FLOWERS INCLUDING BLUISH PURPLE

❧

FLOWERS SYMMETRICAL, WITH 3 PETALS OR PETAL-LIKE PARTS

LEAVES BASAL OR ALTERNATE, SIMPLE

Wild Iris, Blue Flag, Fleur-de-lis

•*Iris versicolor* L.

•Iris family **Iridaceae**

FLOWERING SEASON: June to early July. FLOWERS: violet-blue, several terminal on an upright stem; about 3" (7.5 cm) wide, perianth 6-parted; 3 outer parts broadly paddle-shaped with down-turned tips and yellow and white veining; 3 inner parts smaller, narrower, somewhat erect. PLANT: 2–3' (60–90 cm) tall; leaves basal, simple, long and narrow, margin entire, bluish green. HABITAT: marshes, wet meadows, and along bodies of water. COMMENTS: because most individuals focus on the 3 prominent down-turned petals and tend not to notice the 3 less conspicuous upright petals, we have placed this wildflower in this section.

Spiderwort

•*Tradescantia virginica* L.

•Dayflower family **Commelinaceae**

FLOWERING SEASON: June–July. FLOWERS: blue to purple, rarely white, few, in a compact terminal cluster; 1–2" (2.5–5 cm) wide, with 3 broad petals. PLANT: 8–36" (20–90 cm) tall; leaves alternate, simple, long and narrow, margin entire, green. HABITAT: woodlands and thickets.

FLOWERS SYMMETRICAL, WITH 4 PETALS OR PETAL-LIKE PARTS

LEAVES OPPOSITE, SIMPLE

Fringed Gentian

•*Gentianopsis crinita* (Froel.) Ma

•Gentian family **Gentianaceae**

FLOWERING SEASON: September–October. FLOWERS: blue, several, terminal; about 2" (5 cm) long, tubular with 4 rounded, heavily fringed, apical petal-like lobes. PLANT: about 1–3' (30–90 cm) tall; leaves opposite, simple, lance-shaped with a rounded base, margin entire, green. HABITAT: moist meadows and roadsides.

Bluets

•*Houstonia caerulea* L.

•Madder family **Rubiaceae**

FLOWERING SEASON: early May to mid-June. FLOWERS: pale violet to white with a yellow center, few to several, terminal; about 7/16" (1.1 cm) wide, tubular with 4 sharply pointed, petal-like lobes. PLANT: 3–7" (7.5–17.5 cm) tall; leaves basal and opposite, simple, narrowly paddle-shaped, margin entire, green. HABITAT: open grassy areas, often at higher elevations.

FLOWERS SYMMETRICAL, WITH 5 PETALS OR PETAL-LIKE PARTS

LEAVES BASAL, SIMPLE

Marsh-rosemary, Sea-lavender

•*Limonium carolinianum* (Walt.) Britt.

•Leadwort family **Plumbaginaceae**

FLOWERING SEASON: August–September. FLOWERS: lavender, pale purple, many in a large, loose terminal cluster; tiny, with 5 rounded petals. PLANT: 1–2' (30–60 cm) tall; leaves basal, simple, broadly lance-shaped with a long stalk, margin entire or minutely wavy, green. HABITAT: coastal meadows.

Wild Iris, Blue Flag, Fleur-de-lis / *Iris versicolor*

Bluets / *Houstonia caerulea*

Marsh-rosemary, Sea-lavender / *Limonium carolinianum*

Fringed Gentian / *Gentianopsis crinita*

Spiderwort / *Tradescantia virginica*

LEAVES ALTERNATE, SIMPLE

Forget-me-not
•*Myosotis scorpioides* L.
•Borage family **Boraginaceae**
FLOWERING SEASON: May–July. FLOWERS: pale blue with a yellow center, many, in long, slender clusters; about ¼" (6 mm) wide, with 5 nearly round, petal-like lobes. PLANT: 6–18" (15–45 cm) tall; leaves alternate, simple, oblong, minutely hairy, margin entire, green. HABITAT: along brooks and in marshes and drainage ditches.

Creeping Bellflower
•*Campanula rapunculoides* L.
•Bluebell family **Campanulaceae**
FLOWERING SEASON: late June to early August. FLOWERS: blue to violet, many in a slender 1-sided terminal cluster; about 1¼" (3.1 cm) long, bell-shaped with 5 somewhat flaring triangular lobes. PLANT: about 1–3' (30–90 cm) tall; leaves alternate, simple, broadly lance-shaped, margin toothed, green. HABITAT: fields, roadsides, and waste areas.

Harebell, Bluebell
•*Campanula rotundifolia* L.
•Bluebell family **Campanulaceae**
FLOWERING SEASON: late June–August. FLOWERS: blue, few to several, in slender 1-sided upper axial clusters; up to 1" (2.5 cm) long, bell-shaped with 5 triangular lobes. PLANT: 6–39" (15–97.5 cm) or more tall; leaves basal and alternate, simple, basal leaves broadly heart-shaped; stem leaves very narrow, green. HABITAT: moist, rocky areas.

Venus' Looking Glass
•*Triodanis perfoliata* (L.) Nieuwl.
•Bluebell family **Campanulaceae**
FLOWERING SEASON: mid-June to mid-August. FLOWERS: blue to violet, several along an erect stem; about ¾" (1.9 cm) wide, bell-shaped with 5 pointed petal-like lobes. PLANT: 6–24" (15–60 cm) tall; leaves alternate, simple, broadly ovate, sessile, margin toothed, green. HABITAT: dry woods and meadow margins.

LEAVES ALTERNATE, DEEPLY LOBED

Nightshade
•*Solanum dulcamara* L.
•Nightshade family **Solanaceae**
FLOWERING SEASON: early June into August. FLOWERS: purple, blue, or white with a protruding yellow center, several, in loose clusters; about ½" (1.3 cm) wide, corolla with 5 deeply recurved, sharply pointed petal-like lobes, often nodding. PLANT: vine-like, 2–8' (0.6–2.4 m) long; leaves alternate, simple, 3-lobed; central lobe large, broadly tear-shaped; lateral lobes small and lance-shaped; margin entire, green; fruit green to bright red when ripe, tomato-like, *poisonous*. HABITAT: roadsides, waste areas, and thickets. COMMENTS: often found bearing flowers and fruit simultaneously.

LEAVES OPPOSITE, SIMPLE

Common Periwinkle
•*Vinca minor* L.
•Dogbane family **Apocynaceae**
FLOWERING SEASON: late April–May. FLOWERS: blue or occasionally white or pinkish, few, solitary in axils; about 1" (2.5 cm) wide, with 5 wide, blunt, petal-like parts. PLANT: prostrate, stems 6–24" (15–60 cm) long; leaves opposite, simple, oblong, margin entire, green. HABITAT: escaped from cultivation into woodlands and meadows.

Harebell, Bluebell / *Campanula rotundifolia*

Venus' Looking Glass / *Triodanis perfoliata*

Creeping Bellflower / *Campanula rapunculoides*

Forget-me-not / *Myosotis scorpioides*

Nightshade / *Solanum dulcamara*

Common Periwinkle / *Vinca minor*

Blue Phlox
- *Phlox divaricata* L.
- Phlox family **Polemoniaceae**

FLOWERING SEASON: mid-May to mid-June. FLOWERS: blue, several to many in a rounded terminal cluster; about 1" (2.5 cm) wide, tubular with 5 paddle-shaped, petal-like lobes. PLANT: 12–20" (30–50 cm) tall; leaves opposite, simple, lance-shaped, margin entire, green. HABITAT: woodlands.

Blue Vervain
- *Verbena hastata* L.
- Verbena family **Verbenaceae**

FLOWERING SEASON: July to early September. FLOWERS: blue, many, in slender terminal clusters; about ⅛" (3 mm) wide, tubular with 5 tiny lobes. PLANT: 3–7' (0.9–2.1 m) tall; leaves opposite, simple, lance-shaped, margin toothed, green. HABITAT: moist fields, meadows, and drainage ditches.

FLOWERS SYMMETRICAL, WITH 6 PETALS OR PETAL-LIKE PARTS

LEAVES BASAL, SIMPLE

Blue-eyed Grass
- *Sisyrinchium angustifolium* Mill.
- Iris family **Iridaceae**

FLOWERING SEASON: late May–June. FLOWERS: violet-blue with a yellow center, 1–3, terminal on an upright 2-edged stem; about ¾" (1.9 cm) wide, perianth with 6 oblong, bristle-tipped petal-like parts. PLANT: 3–14" (7.5–35 cm) tall; leaves basal, simple, long and narrow, margin entire, green; flowering stem with a long, leaf-like bract halfway up the stem. HABITAT: moist fields and meadows.

FLOWERS SYMMETRICAL, WITH 7 OR MORE PETALS OR PETAL-LIKE PARTS

LEAVES ALTERNATE, SIMPLE

Chicory
- *Cichorium intybus* L.
- Aster family **Asteraceae**

FLOWERING SEASON: mid-June to mid-September. FLOWERHEADS: blue or occasionally white, many, in clusters of 1–4 along the branching stems; individual flowerheads about 1¼" (3.1 cm) wide, rimmed with many oblong, minutely 5-toothed petal-like rays. PLANT: 1–3' (30–90 cm) tall; leaves basal and alternate, simple, lance-shaped, margin unevenly toothed, green. HABITAT: fields, roadsides, and waste areas.

Blue Wood Aster
- *Aster cordifolius* L.
- Aster family **Asteraceae**

FLOWERING SEASON: September–October. FLOWERHEADS: white, violet, or blue, with a pinkish to purplish center, many, terminal and upper axial; individual flowerheads ½–¾" (1.3–1.9 cm) wide, rimmed with 10–20 petal-like rays. PLANT: 1–5' (0.3–1.5 m) tall; leaves alternate and basal; upper leaves lance-shaped; lower and basal leaves heart-shaped with a deeply cleft base, margin toothed, green. HABITAT: woods and thickets.

Blue Wood Aster / *Aster cordifolius*

Blue Phlox / *Phlox divaricata*

Blue-eyed Grass / *Sisyrinchium angustifolium*

Blue Vervain / *Verbena hastata*

Chicory / *Cichorium intybus*

FLOWERS NOT RADIALLY SYMMETRICAL; MINUTE, FILAMENTOUS, TUBULAR WITH NO PETAL-LIKE LOBES, OR WITH NO OBVIOUS PETAL-LIKE PARTS

LEAVES BASAL, SIMPLE

Pickerel-weed
•*Pontederia cordata* L.
•Pickerel-weed family **Pontederiaceae**
FLOWERING SEASON: late July–August.
FLOWERS: blue, many on a densely flowered 1–3" (2.5–7.5 cm) long cylindrical terminal cluster; about ½" (1.3 cm) wide, perianth tubular and 2-lipped, each lip with 3 long petal-like lobes; the central lip of the upper lobe with 2 large yellow spots. PLANT: 1–4' (0.3–1.2 m) tall; leaves mostly basal, simple, narrowly heart-shaped, margin entire, green. HABITAT: aquatic, in the shallow borders of ponds and streams.

Great Spurred Violet, Selkirk Violet
•*Viola selkirkii* Pursh ex Goldie
•Violet family **Violaceae**
FLOWERING SEASON: May. FLOWERS: violet, several, on individual stalks; about ½" (1.3 cm) wide, with 5 unequal rounded petals and a thick, blunt spur at the base. PLANT: 1½–4" (3.8–10 cm) tall; leaves basal, simple, broadly ovate to nearly round with a deeply cleft, heart-shaped base, margin finely toothed, green. HABITAT: moist woodlands.

Bird's-foot Violet
•*Viola pedata* L.
•Violet family **Violaceae**
FLOWERING SEASON: April–September.
FLOWERS: lilac to bluish with a white center surrounding short protruding orange stamens, few to several on individual stalks; about 1–1½" (2.5–3.8 cm) wide, with 5 unequal, rounded petals. PLANT: 3–10" (7.5–25 cm) tall; leaves basal, simple but deeply divided into 5–11 narrow palmate lobes, green.

HABITAT: fields and woodlands.

LEAVES ALTERNATE, SIMPLE

Long-spurred Violet
•*Viola rostrata* Pursh
•Violet family **Violaceae**
FLOWERING SEASON: May. FLOWERS: pale violet with blue veining, several, terminal; about ¾" (1.9 cm) wide, with 5 unequal rounded petals and a long, slender spur at the base. PLANT: 2–7" (5–17.5 cm) tall; leaves basal and alternate, simple, somewhat heart-shaped, margin toothed, green. HABITAT: woodlands.

Viper's Bugloss
•*Echium vulgare* L.
•Borage family **Boraginaceae**
FLOWERING SEASON: mid-June to mid-August. FLOWERS: bright blue to purplish, several to many in tall, slender clusters; up to 1" (2.5 cm) long, tubular with 5 unequal rounded lobes. PLANT: 12–30" (30–75 cm) tall; leaves alternate, simple, narrowly oblong, hairy, margin entire, green. HABITAT: fields and waste areas.

Blue Toadflax
•*Linaria canadensis* (L.) Dumort
•Figwort family **Scrophulariaceae**
FLOWERING SEASON: May–September.
FLOWERS: pale blue, several to many, alternate in a slender terminal cluster; about ¼" (6 mm) long, tubular, 2-lipped with a hook-shaped, slender spur at the base; upper lip with 2 erect petal-like lobes; lower lip with 3 larger, spreading petal-like lobes. PLANT: 4–26" (10–65 cm) tall; leaves alternate, simple, long and narrow, margin entire, green. HABITAT: dry, often sandy, soil.

Great Spurred Violet, Selkirk Violet / *Viola selkirkii*

Pickerel-weed / *Pontederia cordata*

Viper's Bugloss / *Echium vulgare*

Blue Toadflax / *Linaria canadensis*

Long-spurred Violet / *Viola rostrata*

Bird's-foot Violet / *Viola pedata*

Great Blue Lobelia
•*Lobelia siphilitica* L.
•Bluebell family **Campanulaceae**
FLOWERING SEASON: August–September.
FLOWERS: bright blue, several to many in a showy slender terminal cluster; up to 1" (2.5 cm) long, tubular at the base, with 3 broad lower lobes and 2 smaller upper lobes. PLANT: 1–3' (30–90 cm) tall; leaves alternate, simple, lance-shaped, margin toothed, green. HABITAT: moist meadows, swamps, and edges of large bodies of water.

Spiked Lobelia
•*Lobelia spicata* Lam.
•Bluebell family **Campanulaceae**
FLOWERING SEASON: July–August. FLOWERS: pale blue, many in a slender terminal cluster; about ⁵⁄₁₆" (8 mm) long, tubular, 2-lipped; upper lip with 2 narrow erect lobes; lower lip with 3 larger, lance-shaped lobes. PLANT: 1–4' (0.3–1.2 m) tall; leaves alternate and basal, simple, oblong to oval, margin wavy, green. HABITAT: sandy soil along woodlands and roadsides. COMMENTS: brook lobelia, *Lobelia kalmii*, found in moist soils along waterways, is pale blue with a white central area on the lower lip. Water lobelia, *L. dortmanna*, which grows in shallow water, has pale blue or whitish flowers and small basal leaves that are frequently submerged.

Dayflower
•*Commelina communis* L.
•Dayflower family **Commelinaceae**
FLOWERING SEASON: July–September.
FLOWERS: blue, solitary to few, terminal, about ½" (1.3 cm) or more wide, with 2 large, erect blue petals and a smaller whitish lower petal. PLANT: erect or somewhat trailing, stems 1–3' (30–90 cm) long; leaves alternate, simple, broadly lance-shaped, margin entire, green. HABITAT: waste areas and meadows.

Sheep's Bit
•*Jasione montana* L.
•Bluebell family **Campanulaceae**
FLOWERING SEASON: July–August. FLOWERHEAD: blue, terminal, rounded, ½–¾" (1.3–1.9 cm) wide, filamentous. PLANT: 12–20" (30–50 cm) tall; leaves alternate, simple, narrow, margin entire, green. HABITAT: open fields and roadsides. COMMENTS: currently found primarily on the coastal plain; the range of this comparatively recent invasive may be expanding.

LEAVES ALTERNATE, COMPOUND

Blue Columbine
•*Aquilegia vulgaris* L.
•Crowfoot family **Ranunculaceae**
FLOWERING SEASON: June. FLOWERS: blue to purple, one to several, terminal; about 1½" (3.8 cm) long with 5 tubular petals, nodding. PLANT: 1–2' (30–60 cm) tall; leaves alternate, compound with 3–9 leaflets; leaflets wedge-shaped and irregularly lobed, green. HABITAT: woodlands, roadsides, and meadows.

Alfalfa
•*Medicago sativa* L.
•Bean family **Fabaceae**
FLOWERING SEASON: June–August. FLOWERS: violet to blue, many, in elongated clusters; about ¼" (6 mm) long, narrowly pea-like. PLANT: 1–2' (30–60 cm) tall; leaves alternate, compound with 3 leaflets; leaflets obovate, margins minutely toothed near the tip, green; fruit a cluster of brown, tightly spiraled pods. HABITAT: fields, meadows, and waste areas.

Dayflower / *Commelina communis*

Sheep's Bit / *Jasione montana*

Alfalfa / *Medicago sativa*

Blue Columbine / *Aquilegia vulgaris*

Spiked Lobelia / *Lobelia spicata*

Great Blue Lobelia / *Lobelia siphilitica*

Cow-vetch
- *Vicia cracca* L.
- Bean family **Fabaceae**

FLOWERING SEASON: mid-June through July. FLOWERS: bluish purple, many, in 1–4" (2.5–10 cm) long, slender, 1-sided axial clusters; up to ½" (1.3 cm) long, narrowly pea-like, slightly nodding. PLANT: trailing vine, 2–4' (0.6–1.2 m) long; leaves alternate, pinnately compound with 18–24 leaflets; leaflets narrowly lance-shaped, margins entire, green. HABITAT: fields and waste areas.

Wild Lupine
- *Lupinus perennis* L.
- Bean family **Fabaceae**

FLOWERING SEASON: mid-May to mid-June. FLOWERS: bicolored, blue and white, sometimes pinkish, many in an erect, cylindrical 6–10" (15–25 cm) tall terminal cluster; about ¾" (1.9 cm) long, pea-like. PLANT: 1–2' (30–60 cm) tall; leaves alternate, palmately compound with 7–11 leaflets; leaflets narrowly lance-shaped, margins entire, green. HABITAT: dry, sandy soil.

LEAVES OPPOSITE, SIMPLE

Bottle Gentian, Closed Gentian
- *Gentiana clausa* Raf.
- Gentian family **Gentianaceae**

FLOWERING SEASON: mid-August to mid-September. FLOWERS: blue, several, usually in a terminal cluster; about 1½" (3.8 cm) long, corolla tubular, club-shaped to bottle-shaped, nearly to completely closed at the tip. PLANT: 1–2' (30–60 cm) tall; leaves usually opposite, often whorled in the upper 2 axils, simple, lance-shaped, margin entire, green. HABITAT: moist meadows and fens.

Stiff Gentian
- *Gentianella quinquefolia* (L.) Small
- Gentian family **Gentianaceae**

FLOWERING SEASON: September–October. FLOWERS: violet to bluish, 3 to several in terminal and upper axillary clusters; about ¾" (1.9 cm) long, tubular with 5 teeth. PLANT: 6–24" (15–60 cm) tall; leaves opposite, simple, ovate, margin entire, green. HABITAT: moist meadows.

Blue Curls
- *Trichostema dichotomum* L.
- Mint family **Laminaceae**

FLOWERING SEASON: July–October. FLOWERS: blue, 1–3 on branch tips; ½–¾" (0.6–1.9 cm) long, tubular, 5-lobed; upper 4 lobes short, lower lobe longer and pendant; stamens prominent, projecting, nearly circularly coiled. PLANT: 6–24" (15–60 cm) tall; leaves opposite on a square stem, oblong to lance-shaped, margin entire, green. HABITAT: dry, semishaded, sandy soils.

Common Skullcap
- *Scutellaria galericulata* L.
- Mint family **Lamiaceae**

FLOWERING SEASON: July–August. FLOWERS: blue, several, in pairs in axils; about 1" (2.5 cm) long, tubular, 2-lipped; upper lip hood-like and arched over the lower lip. PLANT: 1–3' (30–90 cm) tall; leaves opposite on a square stem, simple, lance-shaped, margin toothed, green. HABITAT: swamps and along streams. COMMENTS: several species of skullcaps have been reported from this region. Mad-dog skullcap, *Scutellaria lateriflora*, bears flowers in long, narrow axial clusters.

Cow-vetch / *Vicia cracca*

Blue Curls / *Trichostema dichotomum*

Stiff Gentian / *Gentianella quinquefolia*

Common Skullcap / *Scutellaria galericulata*

Wild Lupine / *Lupinus perennis*

Bottle Gentian, Closed Gentian / *Gentiana clausa*

Gill-over-the-ground

•*Glechoma hederacea* L.
•Mint family **Lamiaceae**
FLOWERING SEASON: late April into July.
FLOWERS: blue to violet, several in axial
clusters; about ¾" (1.9 cm) long, tubular, 2-lipped; upper lip 2-lobed, lower lip
3-lobed. PLANT: prostrate, creeping, up
to 18" (45 cm) long; leaves opposite on a
square stem, simple, kidney-shaped,
margin scalloped, green. HABITAT: waste
areas, woods, thickets, and lawns.

Monkeyflower

•*Mimulus ringens* L.
•Figwort family **Scrophulariaceae**
FLOWERING SEASON: mid-July through
August. FLOWERS: pale violet, few, axial;
about 1" (2.5 cm) long, tubular with 2
spreading lips; upper lip with 2 petal-
like lobes; lower lip with 3 rounded
petal-like lobes. PLANT: 1–3' (60–90 cm)
tall; leaves opposite on a square stem,
simple, lance-shaped, margin toothed,
green. HABITAT: swamps and along
streams.

Bird's-eye Speedwell

•*Veronica persica* Poir.
•Figwort family **Scrophulariaceae**
FLOWERING SEASON: May–June. FLOW-
ERS: a mixture of white and bluish purple with purple veining, many, axial,
long-stalked; about ⁷⁄₁₆" (1.1 cm) wide,
tubular at the base, with 4 large, unequal,
rounded petal-like lobes. PLANT: often
prostrate and forming mats; leaves opposite, simple, ovate, margin toothed,
green. HABITAT: lawns, fields, and waste
areas. COMMENTS: *Veronica chamaedrys*,
also know as bird's-eye speedwell, has
similar flowers, but they are borne on
spike-like terminal clusters.

Monkeyflower / *Mimulus ringens*

Gill-over-the-ground / *Glechoma hederacea*

Bird's-eye Speedwell / *Veronica persica*

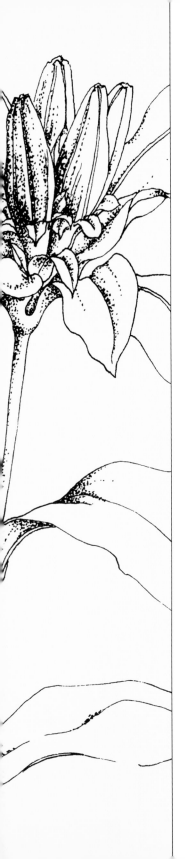

PART SIX

DARK PURPLE
TO BROWN FLOWERS

FLOWERS SYMMETRICAL, WITH 3-4 PETALS OR PETAL-LIKE PARTS

TYPICAL LEAVES LACKING, PARASITIC ON BLACK SPRUCE

Dwarf Mistletoe
•*Arceuthobium pusillum* C. Peck
•Mistletoe family **Viscaceae**
FLOWERING SEASON: late April to early June. **FLOWERS**: brown to greenish brown, many, solitary or paired in axils; dioecious (male and female flowers different, in this species typically found on separate host trees); male flowers about ⅛" (3 mm) wide; female flowers tiny, much smaller than the scale-like leaves; male flowers as large or larger than the scale-like leaves, with 3–4 (occasionally 2) pointed, petal-like divisions, with a bright-yellow stamen at the base of each petal-like part. **PLANT**: parasitic, usually on twigs of black spruce, stem ⅛–¾" (3–19 mm) long; leaves simple, scale-like, nearly round, tiny, tightly appressed to the stem, greenish brown. **HABITAT**: fens and bogs. **COMMENTS**: a black spruce, *Picea mariana*, infected with dwarf mistletoe has much denser foliage than an uninfected tree.

FLOWERS SYMMETRICAL, WITH 3 PETALS OR PETAL-LIKE PARTS

LEAVES BASAL, SIMPLE

Wild Ginger
•*Asarum canadense* L.
•Birthwort family **Aristolochiaceae**
FLOWERING SEASON: late April–May.
FLOWER: brownish purple, solitary, axial; about 1" (2.5 cm) wide, tubular with 3 narrowly triangular, petal-like lobes, lying on or just above the ground.
PLANT: 6–12" (15–30 cm) tall; leaves

paired, appearing basal, simple, kidney-shaped with a pointed tip, long-stalked, margin entire, green. **HABITAT**: woodlands.

FLOWERS SYMMETRICAL, WITH 6 PETALS OR PETAL-LIKE PARTS

LEAVES OPPOSITE, COMPOUND

Blue Cohosh
•*Caulophyllum thalictroides* (L.) Michx.
•Barberry family **Berberidaceae**
FLOWERING SEASON: mid-April into May.
FLOWERS: greenish purple, brownish purple, or yellowish green, several in a loosely flowered cluster; up to ½" (1.3 cm) wide, with 6 petal-like sepals.
PLANT: 1–3' (30–90 cm) tall; leaves opposite with 3 pinnately compound sections; leaflets oval, 3- to 5-lobed, margin entire, green. **HABITAT**: woodlands.

FLOWERS NOT RADIALLY SYMMETRICAL; MINUTE, OR WITH NO OBVIOUS PETAL-LIKE PARTS

TYPICAL LEAVES LACKING

Spotted Coralroot
•*Corallorhiza maculata* (Raf.) Raf.
•Orchid family **Orchidaceae**
FLOWERING SEASON: late July–August.
FLOWERS: greenish purple and white with purple spots, 10–30 in a slender terminal cluster on a purplish to brownish stem; about ½" (1.3 cm) tall and wide, with 5 greenish purple petals and sepals and a white, purple-spotted lip.
PLANT: 8–16" (20–40 cm) tall; leaves lacking. **HABITAT**: woodlands. **COMMENTS**: coralroots are indirect parasites

Dwarf Mistletoe / *Arceuthobium pusillum*

Black Spruce on right, infected by *Arceutho-bium pusillum*; uninfected tree on left

Blue Cohosh / *Caulophyllum thalictroides*

Wild Ginger / *Asarum canadense*

Spotted Coralroot / *Corallorhiza maculata*

that feed on other plants. Early coralroot, *Corallorhiza trifida*, which blooms in June, is the only species with predominantly green coloration.

Autumn Coralroot
- *Corallorhiza odontorhiza* (Willd.) Nutt.
- Orchid family **Orchidaceae**

FLOWERING SEASON: September. **FLOWERS:** greenish purple with a white, purple-spotted lip, 5–15 or more, on a slender terminal cluster; about ⅕" (5 mm) long, with 5 unequal petal-like parts growing from a swollen spherical ovary; in some populations the floral parts remain closed. **PLANT:** 6–15" (15–37.5 cm) tall; leaves lacking. **HABITAT:** woodlands. **COMMENTS:** easily overlooked; the area's smallest coralroot. Obtains nutrients through indirect parasitism of nearby vegetation.

LEAVES BASAL, SIMPLE

Skunk-cabbage
- *Symplocarpus foetidus* (L.) Salisb. ex Nutt.
- Arum family **Araceae**

FLOWERING SEASON: March–April. **FLOWERS:** minute, many on a globular cluster enclosed in a stiff 3–6" (7.5–15 cm) tall hood-shaped sheath that is purple-brown to greenish yellow and often mottled. **PLANT:** 1–2' (30–60 cm) tall; leaves basal, large, simple, broad with protruding veins like those of a cabbage, margin entire, green; unpleasant odor if bruised. **HABITAT:** swamps and moist soil. **COMMENTS:** the flowers, which emerge before the leaves, sometimes bloom through the snow.

LEAVES ALTERNATE, COMPOUND

Groundnut
- *Apios americana* Medik.
- Bean family **Fabaceae**

FLOWERING SEASON: August to mid-September. **FLOWERS:** brownish purple, many, in dense axial clusters; about ½" (1.3 cm) long, pea-like; fragrant. **PLANT:** vine-like, 3–8' (0.9–2.4 m) long; leaves alternate, pinnately compound with 5–7 leaflets; leaflets ovate, margins entire, green. **HABITAT:** moist thickets and meadows.

Skunk-cabbage / *Symplocarpus foetidus*

Groundnut / *Apios americana*

Autumn Coralroot / *Corallorhiza odontorhiza*

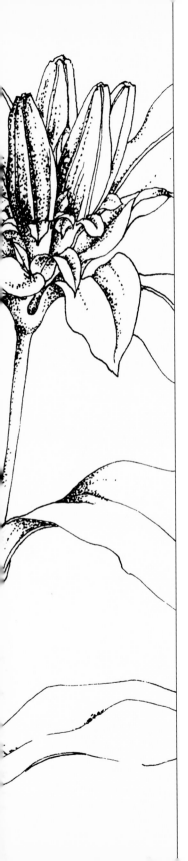

GLOSSARIES AND INDEXES

VISUAL GLOSSARY
GLOSSARY OF TERMS
INDEX OF COMMON NAMES
INDEX OF GENERA
AND SPECIES

VISUAL GLOSSARY

FLORAL PARTS

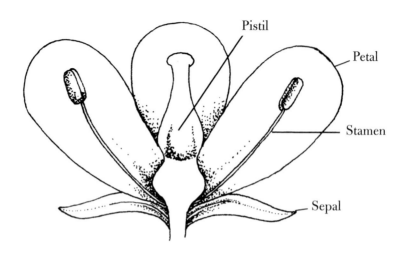

Pistil

Petal

Stamen

Sepal

FLOWER TYPES

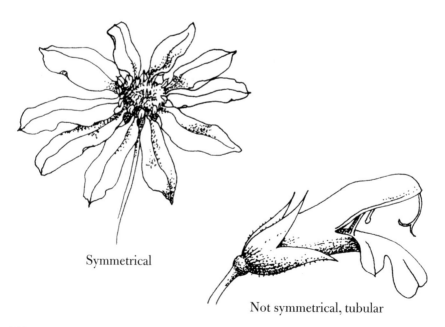

Symmetrical

Not symmetrical, tubular

LEAF TYPES

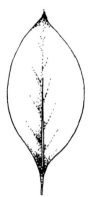

Simple

Pinnately compound

Palmately compound

LEAF PARTS

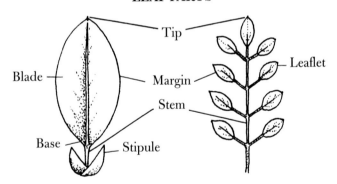

Tip

Leaflet

Blade

Margin

Stem

Base

Stipule

LEAF ARRANGEMENT

Opposite

Alternate

Whorled

Basal

LEAF MARGINS

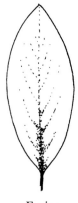

Entire

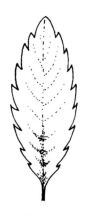

Toothed

Lobed

LEAF TIPS

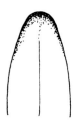

Rounded, blunt

Tapered

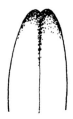

Notched

LEAF AND PETAL BASES

Rounded

Tapered

Heart-shaped

GLOSSARY OF TERMS

ALTERNATE: having leaves arranged singly at different positions along the sides of the stem

APICAL: toward the tip

AXILLARY: located at a leaf-stem juncture

AXIS: the main stem

BASAL: located at the base

BOG: a wet, acidic, nutrient-poor peat land that relies on atmosphere sources for its moisture

BRACT: a small leaf-like structure

CALYX: the basal part of a flower that includes the sepals

COMPOUND: a leaf having two or more leaflets

COROLLA: the apical portion of a flower that includes the petals

DIOECIOUS: having male and female flowers on separate plants

ENTIRE: having a continuous margin unbroken by indentations or teeth

EVERGREEN: a plant retaining most of the leaves through the winter

FEN: a peat land that receives much of its moisture from ground water sources, typically less acidic and richer in nutrients than a true bog

FERTILE: being capable of sexual reproduction

HERBACEOUS: not woody

LEAFLET: one blade-like part of a compound leaf

LOBE: one part of a leaf or flower that is typically rounded

MARGIN: the edge

MARSH: a wetland area with predominantly herbaceous vegetation

NODDING: bending downward

OBLANCEOLATE: pertaining to a leaf that is broadest near the tip

OBLONG: having sides nearly parallel and longer than broad

OBOVATE: egg-shaped, but with the broader end near the tip, the opposite of ovate

OPPOSITE: having leaves arranged in pairs on opposing sides of a stem

OVATE: shaped like an egg, with the broader end at the base

PALMATE: resembling a hand with spread fingers; in a leaf, having divisions radiating out from the center

PENDANT: suspended or hanging down

PERFOLIATE: pertaining to a leaf or leaves with the bases completely surrounding the stem and appearing to be pierced by it

PERIANTH: the combined term for the petals and sepals

PETAL: a usually colorful leaf-like part of the corolla

PINNATE: a leaf with leaflets arranged on opposite sides of the axis, resembling the divisions of a feather

PISTILLATE: referring to either a female flower or the female parts of a complete flower

PROSTRATE: lying flat on the ground

PUBESCENT: coated with short, soft hairs

RAY: the petal-like parts rimming the flowerheads of some species of the Aster family

RECURVED: curved backward or downward

RETICULATION: a net-like pattern

SEPAL: a leaf-like part of the calyx that may be either green or brightly colored

SESSILE: lacking a stalk

SIMPLE: pertaining to a leaf with a single undivided blade

SPATHULATE: shaped like a spoon

SPHERICAL: round or nearly so

SPUR: a tubular extension found on selected flower species, often containing nectar

STAMEN: the male or pollen-producing part of a flower

STAMINATE: referring to either a male flower or the male parts of a complete flower

STEM: the main axis that supports a plant

STERILE: not being capable of sexual reproduction

STIPULE: leaf-like growths found at the bases of leafstalks of roses, wild pansies, and other species

SWAMP: a wetland area typically containing woody vegetation

TERMINAL: located at the tip

TOMENTOSE: having soft matted hairs

TRUNCATE: cut off at one end

VEIN: a small enclosed channel in a leaf or petal through which nutrients and fluids pass

VERNAL POOL/POND: an isolated body of water that most years contains water at least in the spring months, but may dry up later in the summer or fall; such pools or ponds provide essential habitat for many unique wildflowers, and provide breeding sites for fairy shrimp, mole salamanders, and many other amphibians

WASTE AREA: unutilized land typically in proximity to human habitation, frequently a site of organic wastes such as lawn clippings

WHORLED: having leaves arranged in groups of three or more around the same point on a stem

INDEX OF COMMON NAMES

INDEX OF GENERA AND SPECIES

WILLIAM K. CHAPMAN, a biology and science teacher at West Canada Valley Central School and a former member of the adjunct faculty at Utica College of Syracuse University, is an author of *Wildlfowers of New York State in Color*; *Wildflowers of Maine, New Hampshire, and Vermont in Color*; *Orchids of the Northeast, Hickory, Chicory, and Dock* (a wild foods guide); *Plants and Flowers: An Archival Sourcebook; Pheasants under Glass;* and several other nature guides. He is also a contributing author and photographer for *Deer: The Wildlife Series*. His nature photography has appeared in *National Geographic* and the *New York State Conservationist*.

VALERIE CONLEY CHAPMAN was a member of the adjunct faculty at Utica College of Syracuse University. She was an author of *Wildflowers of New York in Color* and *Wildflowers of Maine, New Hampshire, and Vermont in Color*. Her photography has been published in *Birds of the Adirondacks* and *Mammals of the Adirondacks*. Her greatest joys were spending time with her husband, children, and grandchildren, traveling, teaching, and writing. Sadly, she passed away before publication of this volume.

ALAN E. BESSETTE is a professor of biology at Utica College of Syracuse University. He is an author of *Wildlfowers of New York State in Color*; *Wildflowers of Maine, New Hampshire, and Vermont in Color*; *Plants and Flowers: An Archival Sourcebook, Trees and Shrubs of the Adirondacks; Birds of the Adirondacks;* and several books on mushrooms including *Edible Wild Mushrooms of North America, Mushrooms of North America in Color: A Field Guide Companion to Seldom-Illustrated Fungi*, and *Mushrooms of Northeastern North America*

ARLEEN RAINIS BESSETTE is a mycologist and botanical photographer. She is author of *Wildlfowers of New York State in Color*; *Wildflowers of Maine, New Hampshire, and Vermont in Color;* and several books on mushrooms, including *Taming the Wild Mushroom: A Culinary Guide to Market Foraging; Mushrooms of North America in Color;* and *Mushrooms of Northeastern North America*. Arleen has won several national awards for her photography and teaches courses in mycology for the North American Mycological Association and other organizations.